SpringerBriefs in Computer Science

Series Editors

Stan Zdonik
Peng Ning
Shashi Shekhar
Jonathan Katz
Xindong Wu
Lakhmi C. Jain
David Padua
Xuemin Shen
Borko Furht
V. S. Subrahmanian
Martial Hebert
Katsushi Ikeuchi
Bruno Siciliano

For further volumes:
http://www.springer.com/series/10028

Alejandro C. Frery · Talita Perciano

Introduction to Image Processing Using R

Learning by Examples

 Springer

Alejandro C. Frery
Instituto de Computação
Universidade Federal de Alagoas
Maceió, Alagoas
Brazil

Talita Perciano
Instituto de Matemática e Estatística
Universidade de São Paulo
São Paulo, São Paulo
Brazil

ISSN 2191-5768   ISSN 2191-5776 (electronic)
ISBN 978-1-4471-4949-1   ISBN 978-1-4471-4950-7 (eBook)
DOI 10.1007/978-1-4471-4950-7
Springer London Heidelberg New York Dordrecht

Library of Congress Control Number: 2013930142

To Enilson
To Lealdo Leite and Rita Leite

Foreword

It is a pleasure to present this welcome addition to the image processing literature, by Drs. Alejandro C. Frery and Talita Perciano. Their book introduces the R language to that community. R is the *de facto* standard among statisticians. This public domain, open source language popularity derives from many features. The authors, my former—and brilliant—students, presented in this short book the essentials for both the newcomer to the field and the more experienced researcher to start programming in R, by learning through examples. The fact that image processing techniques owe a lot to probability and statistics reinforces the importance of the book.

São Carlos, SP, Brazil   Nelson D. A. Mascarenhas
October 2012

Preface

Thus the man who is responsive to artistic stimuli
reacts to the reality of dreams as does the philosopher
to the reality of existence; he observes closely, and he
enjoys his' observation: for it is out of these images
that he interprets life, out of these processes that he
trains himself for life

Friedrich Nietzsche

This book started as a bunch of files with R code for reading, processing, and saving images. The code slowly evolved into sets of lessons, more or less organized by subjects following the subjects presented in class while lecturing on Digital Image Processing at both the undergraduate and graduate levels at the *Universidade Federal de Alagoas* and the *Universidade Federal de Pernambuco*, Brazil.

The authors were invited to give a short course at the *Congresso da Sociedade Brasileira de Computação*, held in Bento Gonçalves, Rio Grande do Sul State, in 2009. During that Congress they first realized the importance of having a book on Digital Image Processing which, instead of presenting only the mathematical aspects of the discipline or just point-and-click operations and results, delved deeply into the computational aspects of the discipline.

That was the starting point of a project whose product is this book.

The main objective of this book is to introduce the R statistical software to the image processing community in an intuitive and practical manner. Indeed, R brings interesting statistical and graphical tools which are important and necessary for image processing techniques. Besides, it has been proved in the literature that R is among the most reliable, accurate, and portable statistical softwares in the "market" (considering either free/open source or proprietary). In order to achieve that objective, the concepts and techniques are presented theoretically and as much as possible in practice, as the R codes are presented and explained along the text. The idea is that: having this book in hand and an active R session available, the reader can profit from this exciting learning and programming trip all the way through this book.

Other communities can also take advantage of the material presented here as it can be seen as an introduction to image processing and to R for those who are new to the research field and software.

Chapter 1: "Definitions and Notation", works as a prerequisite for the remaining five chapters which can be read more or less independently. The reader is encouraged to try his own implementation of all the code presented in this book and, in particular, to try to develop faster and optimized programs.

Acknowledgments

Alejandro C. Frery is grateful to Professor Héctor Allende O. for his invitation to give a series of lectures on image processing using R in the Universidad Técnica Federico Santa María, Valparaíso, Chile. The notes prepared for those lectures became the starting point of this book.

Talita Perciano is grateful to Professor Alejandro C. Frery who was the one responsible, 9 years ago, for introducing her to both R and Digital Image Processing. It is an honor to be part of the development of this material during the last years and she is grateful for his invitation to co-author this book.

Acknowledgments

Contents

Acronyms

2D	Two-dimensional
3D	Three-dimensional
BMP	Windows BitMap
CMYK	Cyan, Magenta, Yellow, Black
EDA	Exploratory Data Analysis
EPS	Encapsulated PostScript
HSB	Hue, Saturation, Brightness
HSI	Hue, Saturation, Intensity
HSV	Hue, Saturation, Value
HTML	HyperText Markup Language
JPEG	Joint Photographic Experts Group
LUT	Look up Table
LZW	Lempel-Ziv-Welch
PBM	Portable BitMap
PCA	Principal Component Analysis
PDF	Portable Document Format
PGM	Portable GrayMap
PGML	Precision Graphics Markup Language
Pixel	Picture element
PNG	Portable Network Graphics
PPM	Portable PixMap
RGB	Red, Green, Blue
SAR	Synthetic Aperture Radar
SVG	Scalable Vectorial Graphics
TIFF	Tagged Image File Format
VML	Vector Markup Language
W3C	World Wide Web Consortium
XML	EXtensible Markup Language

Chapter 1
Definitions and Notation

> *Never be bullied into silence. Never allow yourself to be made a*
> *victim. Accept no one's definition of your life; define yourself.*
>
> Harvey Fierstein

Let us start by looking at very simple cartoon images, i.e., images formed by flat areas. Images whose properties are perfectly known are usually referred to as "phantoms". They are useful for assessing the properties of filters, segmentation, and classification algorithms, since the results can be contrasted to the ideal output. The images shown in Fig. 1.1 are phantoms, since all the relevant information they convey (the areas) is known.

The cartoon shown in Fig. 1.1a presents four disjoint regions, depicted in shades of gray ranging from white to black. It is stored as a 200×200 matrix of integers $\{1, 2, 3, 4\}$. It was used by Mejail et al. (2003) for the quantitative assessment of the classification of Synthetic Aperture Radar (SAR) data. The cartoon presented in Fig. 1.1b shows a hand-made map of an Amazon area. It was first employed by Frery et al. (1999) for the comparison of SAR segmentation algorithms. It is stored as a 480×480 matrix of integers $\{0, \ldots, 9\}$. Frames are used in both cases to identify the images from the background.

What do these phantoms have in common? They have different logical sizes (the dimension of the matrices) and their values range different sets. Despite this, they are shown occupying the same physical dimension and sharing the similar colors (gray shades, in this case).

We, thus, need a formal description of the objects which will be referred to as "images" in order to be able to deal with them in an unambiguous way.

We will deal with images defined on a finite regular grid S of size $m \times n$. Denote this support $S = \{1, \ldots, m\} \times \{1, \ldots, n\} \subset \mathbb{N}^2$. Elements of S are called *sites*, *coordinates* or *positions*, and can be denoted by $(i, j) \in S$, where $1 \leq i \leq m$ is the row, and $1 \leq j \leq n$ is the column. If the coordinates are not necessary, a lexicographic order will be used to index an arbitrary element of S by $s \in \{1, \ldots, mn\}$. Using the convention employed by R for storing data in a matrix, $s = (n-1)j + i$, as illustrated

A. C. Frery and T. Perciano, *Introduction to Image Processing Using R*,
SpringerBriefs in Computer Science, DOI: 10.1007/978-1-4471-4950-7_1,
© Alejandro C. Frery 2013

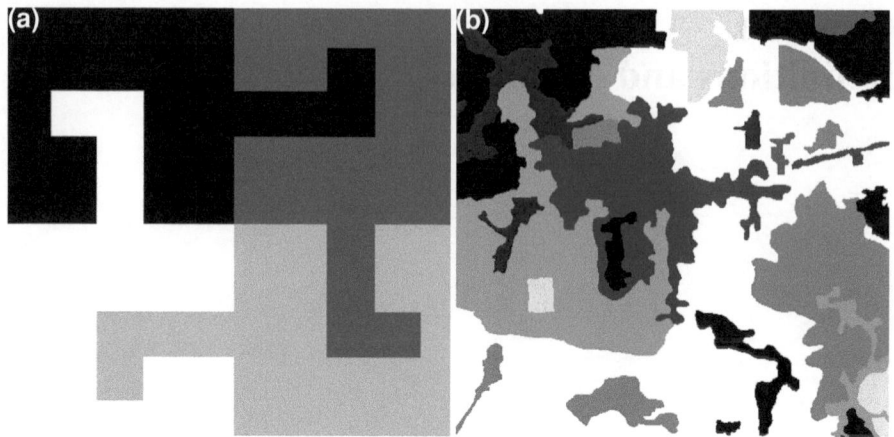

Fig. 1.1 a Cartoon "T", **b** Cartoon "Amazonia" Cartoon images

in the following code where the entries of S, that has $m = 3$ lines and $n = 4$ columns, are the values of the lexicographic order.

```
>  (m  <-  matrix(1:12,  nrow=3))
        [,1]  [,2]  [,3]  [,4]
[1,]      1     4     7    10
[2,]      2     5     8    11
[3,]      3     6     9    12
> m[11]
[1]  11
```

An image is then a function of the form $f: S \to \mathbb{K}$, i.e., $f \in S^{\mathbb{K}}$, where $\mathbb{K}$ the set of possible values in each position. A *pixel* is a pair $(s, f(s))$.

In many situations $\mathbb{K}$ has the form of a Cartesian product, i.e., $\mathbb{K} = K^p$, where p is called the "number of bands" and K is the set of elementary available values.

Images are subjected to storage constraints in practical applications, and, there-fore, the set K is limited to computer words. Examples are the sets which can be described by one bit $\{0, 1\}$ and eight bits $\{0, 1, \ldots, 255\}$, either signed or unsigned integers, floating point and double precision values, and complex numbers in single and double precision.

An image is a mathematical object whose visualization has not been yet defined. A visualization function is an application $v: S^{\mathbb{K}} \to (\mathcal{M}, \mathcal{C})$, where $\mathcal{M}$ is the physical area of the monitor and $\mathcal{C}$ is the set of colors available in that monitor for the software which is being employed (the *palette*). Given an image f, $v(f)$ is a set of spots in the monitor corresponding to each coordinate $s \in S$, where colors are drawn according to the values $f(s)$. It is, therefore, clear that a binary image can be visualized in black and white, in red and blue, or in any pair of colors. . . even the same color. In this last case, the information conveyed by the image is lost in the visualization process, but can be retrieved by switching to a different set of colors.

The well-known zoom operation can be nicely understood using the visualization transformations v_1, v_2 of the binary image $f: \{1, \ldots, 5\} \times \{1, \ldots, 10\} \to \{0, 1\}$. First consider the initial visualization v_1, and assume it makes the "natural" association of $(i, j) \in S$ to the physical coordinates (k, ℓ) of the monitor: $i = k$ and $j = \ell$, and assume it paints 0 and 1 with different colors. A $(2, 2)$ zoom is a visualization function v_2 which, while preserving the color association, maps each $(i, j) \in S$ into four physical coordinates of the monitor, for instance, $\{(2i - 1, 2j - 1), (2i - 1, 2j), (2i, 2j - 1), (2i, 2j)\}$, being the only restriction the availability of physical positions. In this way, there is no need to operate directly on the data, i.e., good image processing platforms (and users) rely on visualization operations whenever possible, rather than on operations that affect the data.

In the following assume we are dealing with real-valued images of a single band, i.e., $\mathbb{K} = \mathbb{R}$. Such images are assumed to have the properties of a linear vector space (see Banon 2000 and the references therein):

- The multiplication of an image f by a scalar $\alpha \in \mathbb{R}$ is an image $g = \alpha f \in S^{\mathbb{R}}$, where $g(s) = \alpha f(s)$ in every $s \in S$.
- The addition of two images f_1, $f_2 \in S^{\mathbb{R}}$ is an image $g = f_1 + f_2 \in S^{\mathbb{R}}$, where $g(s) = f_1(s) + f_2(s)$ in every $s \in S$.
- The neutral element with respect to the addition is the image $\mathbf{0} \in S^{\mathbb{R}}$ defined as $\mathbf{0}(s) = 0$ for every $s \in S$.

These three properties allow the definition of many useful operations, among them

- The negative of the image $f \in S^{\mathbb{R}}$ is the image $g \in S^{\mathbb{R}}$ given by $-f$, i.e., the scalar product of f by -1.
- The difference between two images f_1, $f_2 \in S^{\mathbb{R}}$ is the image $g = f_1 - f_2 \in S^{\mathbb{R}}$.
- The product of two images f_1, $f_2 \in S^{\mathbb{R}}$ is the image $g = f_1 \cdot f_2 \in S^{\mathbb{R}}$ given by $g(s) = f_1(s) f_2(s)$ for every $s \in S$.
- The ratio between f_1 and f_2, provided that $f_s(s) \neq 0$ for every $s \in S$, $g = f_1/f_2$ given by $g(s) = f_1(s)/f_2(s)$.

The assumption that S is finite allows us to define the sum of the image $f \in S^{\mathbb{R}}$ as $\sum f = \sum_{s \in S} f(s)$, and the mean of f as $\overline{f} = \sum f/(mn)$. The inner product between two images f_1, $f_2 \in S^{\mathbb{R}}$ is the scalar given by $\langle f_1, f_2 \rangle = \overline{f_1 \cdot f_2}$. Two images are said to be orthogonal if their inner product is zero, and the norm of $f \in S^{\mathbb{R}}$ is $\|f\| = \sqrt{\langle f, f \rangle}$.

Let us denote $\mathbf{1}$ the constant image $\mathbf{1}(s) = 1$ for every $s \in S$. It is immediate that $\|\mathbf{1}\| = 1$, and that $\overline{f} = \langle f, \mathbf{1} \rangle$.

Local operations, e.g., filters, employ the notion of *neighborhood* which provides a topological framework for the elements of the support S. The neighborhood of any site $s \in S$ is any set of sites that does not include s, denoted $\partial_s \subset S \setminus \{s\}$, obeying the symmetry relationship:

$$t \in \partial_s \iff s \in \partial_t,$$

where "\" denotes the difference between sets, i.e., $A \setminus B = A \cap B^c$, and B^c is the complement of the set B.

Extreme cases of neighborhoods are the empty set $\partial_s = \emptyset$, and all the other sites $\partial_s = S \setminus \{s\} = s^c$. Local operations are typically defined with respect to a relatively small squared neighborhood of odd side ℓ of the form

$$\partial_{(i,j)} = \left(\left(\left[i - \frac{\ell - 1}{2}, i + \frac{\ell - 1}{2}\right] \times \left[j - \frac{\ell - 1}{2}, j + \frac{\ell - 1}{2}\right]\right)\right) \cap S \setminus (i, j),$$
(1.1)

"small" in the sense that $\ell \ll m$ and $\ell \ll n$. Notice that Eq. (1.1) holds for every $(i, j) \in S$, at the expense of reduced neighborhoods close to the edges and borders of the support.

Neighborhoods do not need to be in the form given Eq. (1.1), but this restriction will prove convenient in the forthcoming definitions.

In the following, it will be useful to restrict our attention to certain subsets of images. We will be interested, in particular, in subsets whose indexes are neighborhoods, as defined in Eq. (1.1). Assume $f \in S^{\mathbb{R}}$ is an image, and that $\partial = \{\partial_s : s \in S\}$ is the set of neighborhoods, then $f_{\overline{\partial_s}} : \overline{\partial_s} \to \mathbb{R}$ given by $f_{\overline{\partial_s}}(t) = \{f(t) : t \in \overline{\partial_s}$, where $\overline{\partial_s} = \partial_s \cup \{s\}$ is the closure of ∂_s, is also a real valued image, defined on the grid $\overline{\partial_s}$, for every $s \in S$. We call $f_{\overline{\partial_s}}$ a subimage of the image f with respect to the window $\overline{\partial_s}$. Notice that neighborhoods, which are elements of ∂, do not include s, whereas their closures, i.e., windows, do. The window of (maximum) odd side ℓ around site (i, j) is

$$\partial_{(i,j)} = \left(\left(\left[i - \frac{\ell - 1}{2}, i + \frac{\ell - 1}{2}\right] \times \left[j - \frac{\ell - 1}{2}, j + \frac{\ell - 1}{2}\right]\right)\right) \cap S. \quad (1.2)$$

When all the interest lies on the subimage rather than on the image it comes from, it is also called *a mask*. In this case, the mask can be defined on the support

$$M = \left[-\frac{\ell - 1}{2}, \frac{\ell + 1}{2}\right] \times \left[-\frac{\ell - 1}{2}, \frac{\ell + 1}{2}\right], \quad (1.3)$$

it is said to have (odd) side ℓ, and it is denoted as h_M. Note that $h_M \in M^{\mathbb{R}}$ is an image defined on M.

We will use the indicator function of a set A, defined as

$$\mathbb{1}_A(x) = \begin{cases} 1 \text{ if } x \in A, \\ 0 \text{ otherwise.} \end{cases}$$

A model-based approach with many applications can be found in the book by Velho et al. (2008). The book edited by Barros de Mello et al. (2012) discusses several aspects of image processing and analysis applied to digital documents. Other important references are the works by Barrett and Myers (2004), Jain (1989), Lim (1989), Lira Chávez (2010), Gonzalez and Woods (1992) Myler and Weeks (1993), and Russ (1998) among many others.

1.1 Elements of Probability and Statistics: The Univariate Case

Many of the images we will deal with will be simulated, in the stochastic sense. Also, many of the techniques we will discuss are based upon statistical ideas. It is therefore natural to devote this section to review basic elements of probability, statistics, and stochastic simulation. The book by Dekking et al. (2005) is a good reference for these subjects.

Probability is the branch of mathematics which deals with random experiments: phenomena over which we do not possess complete control but whose set of possible outcomes are known. These phenomena can be repeated as an arbitrary number of times under the same circumstances, and they are observable.

If Ω is the set of all possible outcomes of a random experiment, called the "sample space", denoted by A, B outcomes, i.e., $A, B \subset \Omega$. A "probability" is any specification of values for outcomes $\Pr\colon \Omega \to \mathbb{R}$ having the following properties:

1. Nonnegativity $\Pr(A) \geq 0$ for every $A \subset \Omega$.
2. An outcome is an element of the sample space $\Pr(\Omega) = 1$.
3. Additivity $\Pr(A \cup B) = \Pr(A) + \Pr(B)$ whenever A and B are disjoint, i.e., and $A \cap B = \emptyset$.

Instead of working with arbitrary sets, we will transform every outcome into a set of the real line, say $X\colon \Omega \to \mathbb{R}$. Such transformation, if well defined, is known as "random variable". As possible we can know about a random variable is the probability of any possible event. Such knowledge amounts to saying that we "know the distribution" of the random variable. Among the ways we can know the distribution of the random variable X, one stems as quite convenient: the "cumulative distribution function" which is denoted and defined as

$$F_X(t) = \Pr(X \leq t).$$

There are three basic types of random variables, namely discrete, continuous, and singular. We will only deal with the two former which are defined in the following:

Definition 1.1 (Discrete random variable). Any random variable which maps a finite or countable sample space is discrete.

For convenience but without loss of generality, assume $X\colon \Omega \to \mathbb{Z}$. The distribution of such random variables is also characterized by the "probability vector", that is denoted and given by

$$p_X = \left(\ldots, (-1, \Pr(X = -1)), (0, \Pr(X = 0)), (1, \Pr(X = 1)), \ldots \right)$$
$$= \left(i, \Pr(X = i) \right)_{i \in \mathbb{Z}}.$$

It is clear that $\sum_{i \in \mathbb{Z}} \Pr(X = i) = 1$ by Property 2 above.

Definition 1.2 (Continuous random variable). The random variable X is continuous if exists a function $h\colon \mathbb{R} \to \mathbb{R}_+$ such that $F_X(t) = \int_{-\infty}^{t} h(x)\,dx$ for every $t \in \mathbb{R}$.

If h exists it is called the "density" which characterizes the distribution of X, or just "the density" of X.

Given a function $\Upsilon\colon \mathbb{R} \to \mathbb{R}$, the expected value of the random variable $\Upsilon(X)$, provided the knowledge of the distribution of X, is given by $E(\Upsilon(X)) = \int_{\mathbb{R}} \Upsilon(x)h_X(x)dx$ if the random variable is continuous, and by $E(\Upsilon(X)) = \sum_{\mathbb{Z}} \Upsilon(x) p_X(x)dx$ otherwise, provided the integral or the sum exist. If Υ is the identity function, we have the mean or expected value $E(X)$; if $\Upsilon(X) = E(X^2) - (E(X))^2$ we have the variance.

In the following, we will define basic probabilistic models, i.e., distributions, which will be used in the rest of this book.

Definition 1.3 (Uniform discrete model). A random variable is said to obey the uniform discrete model with $k \geq 1$ states if its distribution is characterized by the probability vector

$$\left(\left(1, \frac{1}{k}\right), \ldots, \left(k, \frac{1}{k}\right)\right).$$

Definition 1.4 (Poisson model). The random variable $X\colon \Omega \to \mathbb{N}$ is said to obey the Poisson model with mean $\lambda > 0$ if the entries of its probability vector are

$$\left(k, e^{-\lambda}\frac{\lambda^k}{k!}\right).$$

Definition 1.5 (Uniform continuous model). The random variable $X\colon \Omega \to [a, b]$, with $a < b$, is said to follow the uniform law on the $[a, b]$ interval if the density which characterizes its distribution is

$$h(x; a, b) = \frac{1}{b - a}\, \mathbb{1}_{[a,b]}(x),$$

where $\mathbb{1}_A$ the indicator function of the set A.

The uniform distribution is central in probability and computational statistics. It is the foundation of the algorithms to generate occurrences of random variables of any type of distribution (see Bustos and Frery 1992 and the references therein).

Definition 1.6 (Beta model). The random variable $X\colon \Omega \to [0, 1]$ obeys the Beta model with parameters $p, q > 0$ if its density is

$$h(x; p, q) = \frac{\Gamma(p + q)}{\Gamma(p)\Gamma(q)}x^{p-1}(1 - x)^{q-1}. \tag{1.4}$$

This situation is denoted as $X \sim B(p, q)$.

If $p = q = 1$ the Beta distribution reduces to the uniform continuous model on the $[0, 1]$ interval. If $p > 1$ and $q > 1$ the mode of this distribution is

$$q_{1/2}(X) = \frac{\alpha - 1}{\alpha + \beta - 2}.$$

This, with the facts that its mean and variance are, respectively,

$$\mu = \mathrm{E}(X) = \frac{p}{p + q}, \tag{1.5}$$

$$\sigma^2 = \mathrm{Var}(X) = \frac{pq}{(p + q)^2(p + q + 1)}, \tag{1.6}$$

gives us a handy model for the simulation of images. Straightforward computation yields that

$$p = \frac{\mu}{1 - \mu} q, \tag{1.7}$$

a handy relation for stipulating the parameters of samples with a fixed desired mean μ.

Definition 1.7 (Gaussian model). The random variable $X : \Omega \to \mathbb{R}$ is said to obey the Gaussian (often also called *normal*) model with mean $\mu \in \mathbb{R}$ and variance $\sigma^2 > 0$ if its density is

$$h(x; \mu, \sigma^2) = \frac{1}{\sqrt{2\pi\sigma^2}} \exp\left\{-\frac{1}{2\sigma^2}(x - \mu)^2\right\},$$

where $\sigma = \sqrt{\sigma^2}$ is known as "standard deviation". If $\mu = 0$ and $\sigma^2 = 1$, it is known as the standard Gaussian distribution.

The main inference techniques we will employ require the knowledge of two elements, defined in the following.

Definition 1.8 (Moment of order k). The moment of order k of the distribution $\mathcal{D}$, characterized either by the probability vector p_X or by the density h_X is given by

$$m_k = \int_{\mathbb{R}} x^k h_X(x) dx \tag{1.8}$$

$$m_k = \sum_{\mathbb{Z}} x^k p_X(x), \tag{1.9}$$

respectively, if the integral or the sum exists.

The basic problem of statistical parameter estimation can be posed as follows. Consider the parametric model $\mathcal{D}(\theta)$, with $\theta \in \Theta \subset \mathbb{R}^p$, where Θ is the parametric space of dimension $p \geq 1$. Assume the random variables $X = (X_1, \ldots, X_n)$ follow this model, and they are independent. The vector $x = (x_1, \ldots, x_n)$ is formed by an observation from each of these random variables. An estimate of θ is a function $\widehat{\theta}(x)$ which we expect will give us an idea of the true but unobserved parameter θ. The estimator $\widehat{\theta}(X)$ is a random variable. One of the most fundamental properties expected from good estimators is the *consistency*: $\lim_{n \to \infty} \widehat{\theta}(X) \to \theta$.

Without loss of generality, in the following we will define the two main estimation techniques only for the continuous case. The reader is referred to the book by Wassermann (2005) for more details and further references.

Definition 1.9 (Estimation by the method of moments). The estimator $\widehat{\theta}$ is obtained by the method of moments if it is a solution of the system of equations

$$f_1(\widehat{\theta}) - \widehat{m}_{i_1} = 0, \tag{1.10}$$

$$\vdots$$

$$f_p(\widehat{\theta}) - \widehat{m}_{i_p} = 0, \tag{1.11}$$

where $f_1, \ldots, f_p$ are linearly independent functions, the left-hand side of Eq. (1.8), and $m_{i_1}, \ldots, m_{i_p}$ are all different sample moments, i.e.,

$$\widehat{m}_j = \frac{1}{n} \sum_{i=1}^n X^j.$$

Definition 1.10 (Estimation by maximum likelihood). The estimator $\widehat{\theta}$ is a maximum likelihood estimator if it satisfies

$$\widehat{\theta} = \arg\max_{\theta \in \Theta} \prod_{i=1}^n h_X(X_i; \theta), \tag{1.12}$$

where the dependence of the density on the parameter θ is explicit.

Since all densities in Eq. (1.12) are positive, we may maximize the logarithm of the product instead.

As will be seen later, R provides routines for computing maximum likelihood estimates in a wide variety of models.

Theorem 1.1 (Transformation by the cumulative distribution function itself). *Let X be a continuous random variable for which the distribution is characterized by the cumulative distribution function F_X. The random variable $U = F_X(X)$ has uniform distribution in $(0, 1)$.*

Definition 1.11 (Empirical function). Consider $x_1, \ldots, x_n$ as occurrences of the random variables $X_1, \ldots, X_n \colon \Omega \to [0, 1]$, where all of them have the same distribution characterized by the cumulative distribution function F. The empirical function, given by

$$\widehat{F}(t) = \frac{1}{n} \#\{i : x_i \leq t\},$$

is an estimator of F.

The properties of the empirical function and its relationship with robust inference can be seen in the classical book of Huber (1981).

Theorem 1.2 (Transformation by inversion). *Let U and $F : \mathbb{R} \longrightarrow [0, 1]$ be an uniform distributed random variable in $(0, 1)$ and the cumulative distribution function of a continuous random variable, respectively. The random variable $Y = F^{-1}(U)$ follows the distribution characterized by F.*

The proof of the Theorem 1.2 and its extension to discrete random variables can be seen in Bustos and Frery (1992).

1.2 From Phantoms to Single Band Images

We already have the necessary apparatus for simulating images. As previously stated, often times the support K of the image is a compact set. In these cases, a precise modeling prevents the use of distributions which are defined on the real numbers $\mathbb{R}$, the positive numbers $\mathbb{R}_+$ and so on.

Consider, for instance, the situation where $K = [0, 1]$. Any Gaussian model for the data will assign a positive probability to events which do not belong to K and, therefore, cannot be considered as image data. In order to circumvent such issue, the data are frequently subjected to a truncation process.

Instead of doing so, we will build images from the phantoms using the Beta model. Consider the phantom presented in Fig. 1.1a. It is composed of four areas, so we choose four equally spaced mean values in the $[0, 1]$ interval: 0.2, 0.4, 0.6, and 0.8. Using the relation given in Eq. (1.7), and fixing $q = 4$, if we want observations with means $\mu_k \in \{.2, .4, .6, .8\}$ we have to sample from the $B(p_k, 4)$ law with $p_k \in \{1, 8/3, 6, 16\}$. These four densities are shown in Fig. 1.2a, while the observed image under this model is shown in Fig. 1.2b.

In the following, we will see how the plot and the figure were produced in R.

R provides a number of tools related to distribution functions. They are gathered together by a prefix, indicating the type of function, and a suffix, associated to the distribution. For instance, for the Beta distribution (presented in Definition 1.6), R provides the functions dbeta (density function, as expressed in Eq. 1.4, pbeta (cumulative distribution function), qbeta(quantiles), andrbeta (simulation of Beta deviates). Instead of building our own density function, we will use the one provided by R.

The code is presented in Listing 1.1. Line 1 builds a vector with 500 equally spaced elements, starting in zero and ending in one; this will be the abscissa of all densities. Lines 2 and 3 draw the first Beta density with $p = 16$ and $q = 4$; it also

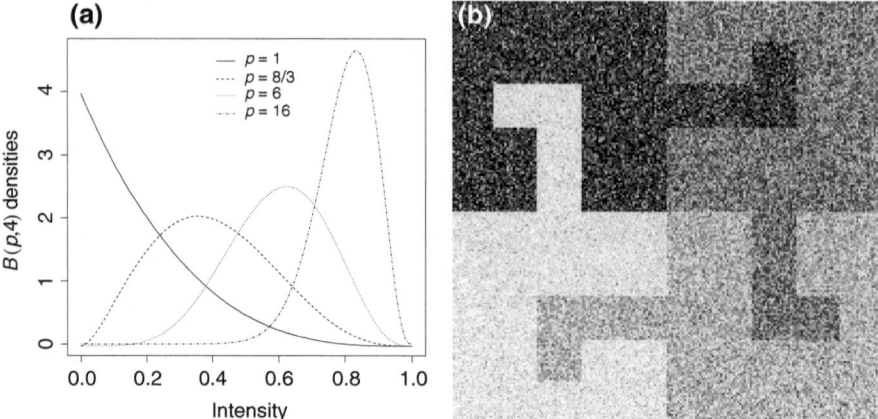

Fig. 1.2 **a** Beta densities. **b** Phantom under the Beta model Four Beta densities and observed image under the Beta model

sets the labels (notice the use of the `expression` command). We start by this curve because it is the one which spans the largest ordinates interval. Lines 7–9 produce the legend.

Listing 1.1 Drawing Beta densities

```
1  x <- seq(0, 1, length=500)
2  curve(dbeta(x, 16, 4), lty=4, xlab="Intensity",
3         ylab=expression(italic(B)(italic(p), 4) * " densities") )
4  curve(dbeta(x, 6, 4), add=TRUE, lty=3)
5  curve(dbeta(x, 8/3, 4), add=TRUE, lty=2)
6  curve(dbeta(x, 1, 4), add=TRUE, lty=1)
7  legend(x="top", expression(italic(p) == 1, italic(p) == 8/3,
8         italic(p) == 6, italic(p) == 16), bty="n",
9         lty=1:4)
```

The example presented in Listing 1.1 is not a paradigm of economic R code. All codes presented in this book place readability in front of elegance and economy. The reader is strongly encouraged to try it, experimenting the countless possibilities the language offers.

The T phantom is available in the `Timage.Rdata` file. Listing 1.2 shows how to read this phantom and to produce the image shown in Fig. 1.2b. Line 1 reads the data which stores the phantom, and Line 2 checks the unique values in this matrix; they are 1, 2, 3, and 4. Line 3 makes a copy of the phantom in a new variable (`TBeta`) which will be the sampled image; this spares the effort to discover and set the dimensions of the output. Lines 4–7 sample from each Beta distribution the correct number of observations (`200*200/4`, since each class occupies exactly one fourth of the phantom), with the desired parameters. Line 8 transforms the data matrix into an image, which can be visualized with the command `plot`.

Listing 1.2 Reading the phantom and producing the beta image

```
1  load("../Images/Timage.Rdata")
2  unique(sort(T))
3  TBeta <- T
4  TBeta[which(T == 1)] <- DarkestBeta <- rbeta(200*200/4, 1, 4)
5  TBeta[which(T == 2)] <- rbeta(200*200/4, 8/3, 4)
6  TBeta[which(T == 3)] <- rbeta(200*200/4, 6, 4)
7  TBeta[which(T == 4)] <- BrightestBeta <- rbeta(200*200/4, 16, 4)
8  plot(imagematrix(TBeta))
```

Notice that the data in the darkest and brightest areas have been stored in the variables `DarkestBeta` and `BrightestBeta`, respectively, for future use.

In this example, we worked within the [0, 1] interval, so there is no need to further transform the data to fit into the `imagematrix` restriction. Had we used the Gaussian distribution or any other probability law with a noncompact support, such transformation would have been mandatory, as will be seen in the next example.

The Gaussian model presented in Definition 1.7 (p. x) is the most notorious and overall employed statistical model, mainly due to historical reason and to the fact that it has nice mathematical properties. Many image processing techniques rely on the Gaussian hypothesis. We built the image presented in Fig. 1.2b by fixing one of the parameters of the Beta distribution and choosing the desired mean; the other parameter, and the variance, are a consequence of this choice. In the following, we will use the Gaussian model to freely stipulate the mean and the variance of data in each region.

Figure 1.3 presents the Gaussian model and an image produced by it. The similarity between Figs. 1.2b and 1.3b is striking, albeit the models are quite different, as can be seen comparing Figs. 1.2a and 1.3a. This is due to the inability of the human eye to perceive statistics beyond the first moment, i.e., the mean; since the means in each region under the Beta and the Gaussian model are equal, it is quite hard to tell them apart.

As in the Beta model example, the data in the darkest and brightest areas have been stored in the variables `DarkestGaussian` and `BrightestGaussian`, respectively. Later we will see how to take samples by interactively choosing areas in an image, but direct attribution, as seen here, suffices for the moment. In the following we will analyze these data, including a fit to their models.

Listing 1.3 presents the descriptive analysis of the darkest and brightest areas from both the Beta and Gaussian models. First, we fix the number of decimal digits of the output to two (line 1). Second, a `summary` command is issued for each data set. This command produces as output the minimum, first quantile, median, mean, third quartile, and maximum values of its input. In this listing, we mix both input and output in R; the former is prefixed by the ">" symbol. It is noticeable that the means coincide in both regions, but all other quantities differ. Lines 14–16 store the four variables in a very convenient R structure: a `dataframe`; this is done also by fixing the name of each variable to a mnemonic pair of characters. Lines 17 and 18 produce the boxplot shown in Fig. 1.4. The option `notch=TRUE` adds a graphical

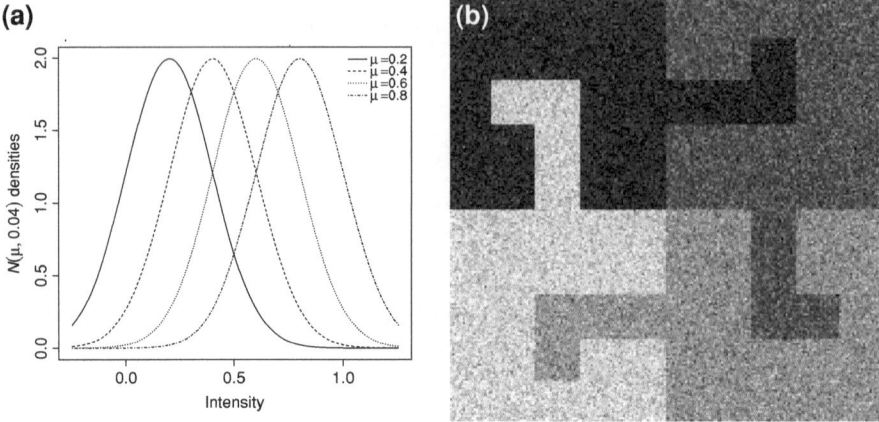

Fig. 1.3 a Gaussian densities. **b** Phantom under the Gaussian model Four Gaussian densities and observed image under the Gaussian model

representation of the confidence interval of each median which, in this case, suggest the differences are not random. The asymmetry of the data from the dark Beta model is evident in this plot, as well as the different spread of the data around the medians. Details about this plot can be found in the book by Dekking et al. (2005).

Listing 1.3 Descriptive analysis of data from the darkest and brightest areas

```
1  > options(digits=2)
2  > summary(DarkestBeta)
3     Min. 1st Qu.  Median    Mean 3rd Qu.    Max.
4     0.00    0.07    0.16    0.20    0.29    0.91
5  > summary(DarkestGaussian)
6     Min. 1st Qu.  Median    Mean 3rd Qu.    Max.
7    -0.21    0.13    0.20    0.20    0.27    0.54
8  > summary(BrightestBeta)
9     Min. 1st Qu.  Median    Mean 3rd Qu.    Max.
10    0.33    0.74    0.81    0.80    0.86    0.99
11 > summary(BrightestGaussian)
12    Min. 1st Qu.  Median    Mean 3rd Qu.    Max.
13    0.45    0.73    0.80    0.80    0.86    1.13
14 > DarkestBrightest <- data.frame(DB <- DarkestBeta,
15    DG <- DarkestGaussian,  BB <- BrightestBeta,
16    BG <- BrightestGaussian)
17 > boxplot(DarkestBrightest, horizontal=TRUE, notch=TRUE,
18    names=c("DB", "DG", "BB", "BG"), xlab="Intensities")
```

So far we made a very simple descriptive analysis of the data contained in the image shown in Fig. 1.2b, assuming that we have labels for each value, i.e., that we know the class it comes from. This descriptive analysis consisted in calling the summary function and in drawing boxplots and histograms, but Exploratory Data

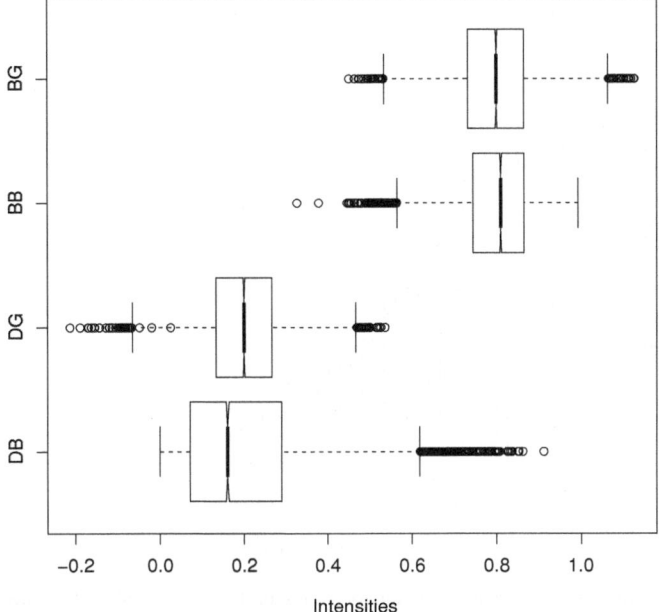

Fig. 1.4 Boxplots of the darkest and brightest data from the Beta and Gaussian models

Analysis—EDA, originated by Tuckey (1973), is a well established and growing speciality of statistics which offers much more.

EDA lets the data speak for themselves, without strong assumptions about the underlying distributions and relationships among them. It is more a collection of tools, both graphical and quantitative, than a formal approach. EDA practitioners are guided by intuition and results, rather than by established recipes. Every sound data analysis in image processing (and in any other area) should be preceded careful and as exhaustive as possible EDA. Unfortunately, this is seldom seen in the literature.

One step further consists in assuming a parametric model and estimating the parameters using the available data. Assume the data came from the Beta distribution; the code presented in Listing 1.4 shows how to estimate the parameters by maximum likelihood. Line 1 reads the MASS library which provides the fitdistr function. This function fits univariate data to parametric models, offering flexibility to fix or constraint the parameters. The model can be one of a comprehensive list of predefined distributions (which includes the Beta, the Gaussian and other important probability laws), or it can be specified through a density or probability function. It requires a starting point for the search of the estimates, which is provided by means of a named list (see Line 2). Upon a successful call, the function fitdistr returns an R object containing the parameter estimates, their estimated standard errors, the estimated variance-covariance matrix, the value of the log-likelihood function at the estimates; only the first two are shown by default, as seen in lines 5 and 6. Lines 7 and 8 extract

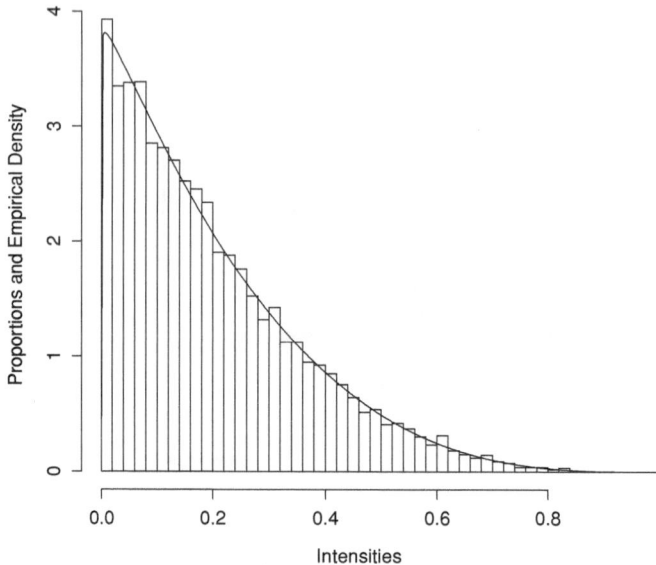

Fig. 1.5 Histogram and empirical Beta density for the darkest region of the Beta image

the estimates from the object and assign them to mnemonic variables. Notice that the estimates $(\widehat{p}, \widehat{q}) = (1.017, 4.090)$ and the true values $(p, q) = (1, 4)$ are very close, and even closer when we notice that the observed bias (the difference between the true and estimated values) is within less than two observed standard deviations. The estimated parameters will be now used to draw the empirical (estimated) density over the histogram. This will serve as a visual assessment of the quality of the model. Lines 9–11 compute and plot the histogram of the data using the Friedman-Diakonis (breaks="FD") algorithm for computing the points at which the breaks are. Line 12 computes and adds the empirical density to the proportions histogram, showing how similar they are. The result of running this piece of code is shown in Fig. 1.5.

Listing 1.4 Maximum likelihood estimation of the parameters of the Beta distribution

```
1  > library(MASS)
2  > (DarkestParameters <- fitdistr(DarkestBeta, "beta",
3      start=list(shape1=1, shape2=1)))
4      shape1    shape2
5      1.017     4.090
6     (0.013)   (0.061)
7  > pd <- DarkestParameters$estimate[1]
8  > qd <- DarkestParameters$estimate[2]
9  > hist(DarkestBeta, xlab="Intensities",
10     ylab="Proportions and Empirical Density",
11     main="", breaks="FD", probability=TRUE)
12 > curve(dbeta(x, pd, qd), from=0, to=1, add=TRUE, n=500)
```

The reader is invited to repeat this analysis using the data from the brightest region.

1.3 Multivariate Statistics

We have dealt with images with a single band, but multiband imagery is also treated in this book (these concepts are defined in the next section). While, as already seen, the former can be described with univariate random variables, the latter require multivariate models.

Definition 1.12 (Multivariate random variables). A random vector is a function $X : \Omega \to \mathbb{R}^m$ such that each component is a random variable.

The distribution of the random vector $X = (X_1, \ldots, X_m)$ is characterized by the multivariate cumulative distribution function:

$$F_X(x_1, \ldots, x_m) = \Pr(X_1 \leq x_1, \ldots, X_m \leq x_m).$$

If there is a function h_X such that

$$F_X(x_1, \ldots, x_m) = \int_{-\infty}^{x_1} \cdots \int_{-\infty}^{x_m} h_X(t_1, \ldots, t_m) dt_1 \ldots dt_m,$$

then the random vector X is said to be continuous, and h_X is the density which characterizes its distribution. Although there are plenty of discrete multivariate distributions (c.f. the book by Johnson et al. 1997 and the references therein), for the purposes of this book it will suffice to consider continuous random variables. In particular, the only continuous multivariate distribution we will employ in this book is the Gaussian law. More continuous multivariate distributions can be found in the book by Kotz et al. (2000).

We need new definitions of the mean and the variance when dealing with multivariate distributions. The vector of means (or mean vector) of $X : \Omega \to \mathbb{R}^m$ is

$$E(X) = (E(X_1), \ldots, E(X_m)),$$

provided it exists. The covariance matrix of the random vector is $\Sigma = (\sigma_{ij})_{1 \leq i, j \leq m}$, the $m \times m$ matrix whose elements are the covariances $\sigma_{i,j} = \text{Cov}(X_i, X_j)$, provided they exist. The diagonal elements $(\sigma_{ii})_{1 \leq i \leq m}$ are the variances $\sigma_{ii} = \text{Var}(X_i)$.

Provided all the elements of the covariance matrix Σ exist, the correlation matrix $\varrho = (\varrho)_{1 \leq ij \leq m}$ is given by the $m \times m$ correlation coefficients

$$\varrho_{ij} = \frac{\text{Cov}(X_i, X_j)}{\sqrt{\text{Var}(X_i)\text{Var}(X_j)}};$$

clearly, $\varrho_{ii} = 1$ for every $1 \leq i \leq m$. If Σ is positive definite, then $-1 < \varrho_{ij} < 1$, and if $\varrho_{ij} = 0$ we say that X_i and X_j are uncorrelated.

Definition 1.13 [(Proper) multivariate Gaussian distribution]. Consider the vector $\mu \in \mathbb{R}^m$ and the positive definite matrix Σ. The random vector $X : \Omega \to \mathbb{R}^m$

obeys the m-variate Gaussian distribution if the density which characterizes its distribution is

$$f_X(x) = \frac{1}{(2\pi)^{m/2}\sqrt{|\Sigma|}} \exp\left\{ -\frac{1}{2}(x - \mu)^\top \Sigma^{-1}(x - \mu)\right\} \qquad (1.13)$$

where $\top$ denotes transposition, and $|\Sigma|$ is the determinant of the matrix Σ. The vector μ is the vector of means, and Σ is the covariance matrix.

The maximum likelihood estimators of μ and Σ based on a sample of size n of independent and identically distributed multivariate Gaussian random variables $X_1, \ldots, X_n$ are, respectively

$$\widehat{\mu} = \frac{1}{n}\sum_{i=1}^{n} X_i, \text{ and } \widehat{\Sigma} = \frac{1}{n}\sum_{i=1}^{n}(X_i - \widehat{\mu})^\top(X_i - \widehat{\mu}). \qquad (1.14)$$

The multivariate Gaussian distribution is a commodity of image processing software: most algorithms assume it holds, and are therefore based on procedure which produce optimal results under this assumption. The assumption itself is seldom checked in practice.

A practical consequence of assuming the multivariate Gaussian model for the random vector $X: \Omega \to \mathbb{R}^m$ is that if it holds, then every component $(X_i)_{1 \leq i \leq m}$ obeys a Gaussian distribution. R provides a number of routines for checking the goodness-of-fit to arbitrary distributions (among them the well-known χ^2 and Kolmogorov-Smirnov tests), but also a specialized one: the Shapiro-Wilk test (Cohen and Cohen 2008). Graphical tools as, for instance, Quantile–Quantile (QQ) plots are also handy tools for checking the quality of a model.

The following result will be useful when dealing with principal component analysis in Chap. 6.

Claim *[Linear transformation of multivariate random variables] Assume $X: \Omega \to \mathbb{R}^m$ is an m-variate random variable with covariance matrix Σ. Let A be an $m \times m$ matrix. The covariance matrix of the random variable AX is $A\Sigma A^\top$.*

1.4 Multiband Images

We conclude this chapter using the cartoon model presented in Fig. 1.1b. In the same way we previously "filled" each area of the cartoon model shown in Fig. 1.1a with samples from univariate distributions, producing the images shown in Figs. 1.2b and 1.3b, we will replace each class in the Amazonia cartoon model by a sample from a multivariate Gaussian random variable whose parameters are constant along each of the ten classes.

Let us start by defining ten mean vectors: three in red, three in green, and three in blue shades, plus a gray tone, detailed as follows:

$$\mu_{R1} = \begin{pmatrix} 0.50 \\ 0.25 \\ 0.25 \end{pmatrix}, \mu_{R2} = \begin{pmatrix} 0.75 \\ 0.50 \\ 0.25 \end{pmatrix}, \mu_{R3} = \begin{pmatrix} 0.75 \\ 0.50 \\ 0.50 \end{pmatrix},$$

$$\mu_{G1} = \begin{pmatrix} 0.25 \\ 0.50 \\ 0.25 \end{pmatrix}, \mu_{G2} = \begin{pmatrix} 0.25 \\ 0.75 \\ 0.25 \end{pmatrix}, \mu_{G3} = \begin{pmatrix} 0.25 \\ 0.75 \\ 0.50 \end{pmatrix},$$

$$\mu_{B1} = \begin{pmatrix} 0.25 \\ 0.25 \\ 0.50 \end{pmatrix}, \mu_{B2} = \begin{pmatrix} 0.25 \\ 0.50 \\ 0.75 \end{pmatrix}, \mu_{B3} = \begin{pmatrix} 0.50 \\ 0.50 \\ 0.75 \end{pmatrix},$$

and $\mu_G (0.50\ 0.50\ 0.50)^{\top}$, respectively. The command for defining μ_{R1} is just Red1 <- c(.50, .25, .25); the others follow immediately.

Also ten covariance matrices were chosen to specify the distribution of the data in each class. In order to avoid tedious typing, which is also prone to errors, we defined a function which accepts the values of three standard deviations and three correlation coefficients, and produces a covariance matrix as output. This function is presented in Listing 1.5.

Listing 1.5 Function which returns a covariance matrix based on three standard deviations and three correlation coefficients

```
1   BuildCovMatrix <- function(s1, s2, s3, r12, r13, r23) {
2
3     CovMatrix <- matrix(rep(0, 9), nrow=3, ncol=3)
4
5     variances <- c(s1^2, s2^2, s3^2)
6
7     for(i in 1:3) CovMatrix[i,i] <- variances[i]
8
9     CovMatrix[1,2] <- CovMatrix[2,1] <- r12*s1*s2
10    CovMatrix[1,3] <- CovMatrix[3,1] <- r13*s1*s3
11    CovMatrix[2,3] <- CovMatrix[3,2] <- r23*s2*s3
12
13    return(CovMatrix)
14  }
```

Line 3 creates a new matrix of size 3×3 filled with zeroes. Line 5 defines the variances as the square of each standard deviation passed in the input. Line 7 assigns each variance to an element in the diagonal of the matrix, while lines 9–11 compute the off-diagonal elements.

The commands presented in Listing 1.6 instantiate the ten covariance matrices employed in our simulation experiment. They are combinations of two values of standard deviation (intense 0.1 and weak 0.07) and to levels of correlation (intense 0.9 and weak 0.3)

Listing 1.6 Defining covariance matrices

```
1  > si <- 0.1
2  > sw <- 0.07
3  > ri <- 0.9
4  > rw <- 0.3
5
6  > CM1  <- BuildCovMatrix(si, si, si, ri, ri, ri)
7  > CM2  <- BuildCovMatrix(si, si, sw, ri, ri, rw)
8  > CM3  <- BuildCovMatrix(si, sw, si, ri, rw, ri)
9  > CM4  <- BuildCovMatrix(sw, si, si, rw, ri, ri)
10 > CM5  <- BuildCovMatrix(si, sw, sw, ri, rw, rw)
11 > CM6  <- BuildCovMatrix(sw, si, sw, rw, ri, rw)
12 > CM7  <- BuildCovMatrix(sw, sw, si, rw, rw, ri)
13 > CM8  <- BuildCovMatrix(sw, sw, sw, rw, rw, rw)
14 > CM9  <- BuildCovMatrix(sw, sw, sw, ri, ri, ri)
15 > CM10 <- BuildCovMatrix(si, si, si, rw, rw, rw)
```

Listing 1.7 presents an excerpt of the code used to simulate the multivariate image using the parameters discussed above. Line 1 reads the input image, which is in PNG format; notice the presence of a fourth band, it is the alpha channel, intended for transparency. Line 5 identifies and presents the values associated to each class in the cartoon model. In order to avoid possible inconsistencies when checking equality between double precision values, we create an integer-valued version of the phantom in the two subsequent lines of code. Line 11 computes the number of pixels in each class; these will be the sample sizes that will be sampled from each distribution. A data structure to store the simulated image is created in line 15. Line 16 stores in a temporary variable, the desired number of observations obtained by sampling from the multivariate Gaussian distribution with the input mean and covariance matrix. Lines 17 and 18 truncate the data to the [0, 1] interval, a limitation imposed by the format we are using. Line 19 assigns the truncated observations to the coordinates which correspond to the class. Lines 16–19 must be repeated for the other nine classes. Finally, the command plot(AmazoniaSim) produces as output the image shown in Fig. 1.6. The reader is invited to try with different mean vectors and covariance matrices, also with different cartoon models.

Listing 1.7 Simulation of the Gaussian multivariate image

```
1  > Amazonia <- readPNG("../Images/Amazonia.png")
2  > dim(Amazonia)
3  [1] 480 480
4  > options(digits=2)
5  > (valoresAmazonia <- sort(unique(as.vector(Amazonia))))
6   [1] 0.020 0.094 0.176 0.271 0.376 0.486 0.608 0.733 0.863 1.000
7  > # Integer version, just in case
8  > IntAmazonia <- Amazonia
9  > for(i in 1:10) IntAmazonia[Amazonia == valoresAmazonia[i]] <- i
10 > # Sample sizes
11 (SampleSizes <- table(IntAmazonia))
12 IntAmazonia
13       1     2     3     4     5     6     7     8     9    10
14 35723 10518 24385  2139 32849 37188  1487   729  6133 79249
15 > AmazoniaSim  <- imagematrix(Amazonia[,,-4])
16 > temp <- mvrnorm(SampleSizes[1], Red1, CM1)
17 > temp[temp < 0] <- 0
18 > temp[temp > 1] <- 1
19 > AmazoniaSim[IntAmazonia == 1] <- temp
```

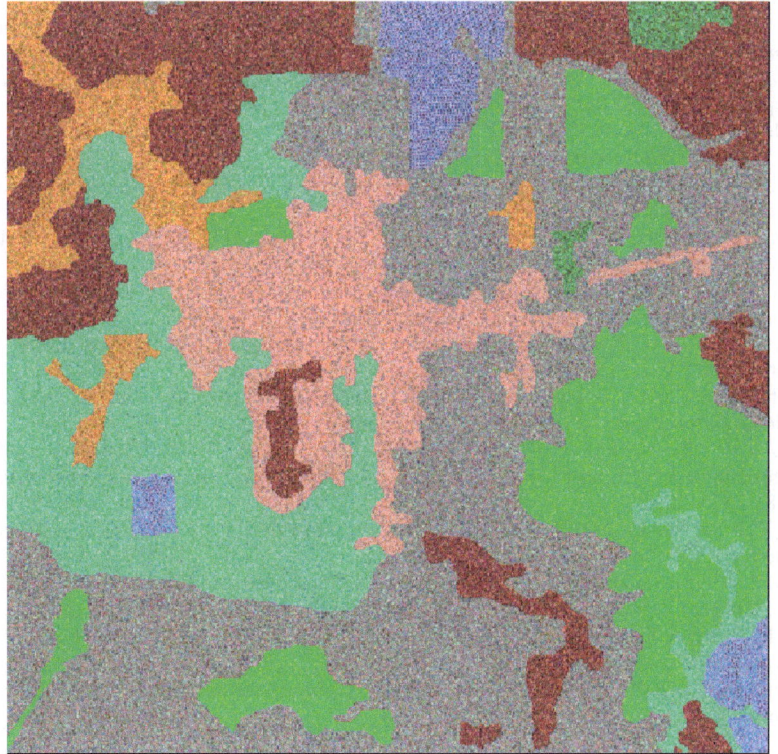

Fig. 1.6 Simulated image with the multivariate Gaussian model and the Amazon cartoon phantom

The reader will notice that not every class shown in the phantom is readily seen in the simulated image. This is due to the confusion induced by the overlapping distributions, a common feature when dealing with real data.

References

Banon, G. J. F. (2000). *Formal introduction to digital image processing*, INPE, São José dos Campos, SP, Brazil. URL http://urlib.net/dpi.inpe.br/banon/1999/06.21.09.31

Barrett, H. H., & Myers, K. J. (2004). *Foundations of image science* (Pure and Applied Optics). Hoboken: Wiley-Interscience.

Barros de Mello, C. A., Oliveira, A. L. I., & Pinheiro dos Santos, W. (2012). *Digital document analysis and processing, Computer Science: Technology and Applications*, New York: Nova Publishers.

Bustos, O. H., & Frery, A. C. (1992). *Simulação estocástica: teoria e algoritmos (versão completa), Monografias de Matemática, 49*. Rio de Janeiro, RJ: CNPq/IMPA.

Cohen, Y., & Cohen, J. Y. (2008). *Statistics and data with R*. New York: Wiley.

Dekking, F. M., Kraaikamp, C., Lopuhaä, H. P., & Meester, L. E. (2005). *A modern introduction to probability and statistics: understanding why and how*. London: Springer.

Frery, A. C., Lucca, E. D. V., Freitas, C. C. & Sant'Anna, S. J. S. (1999). *SAR segmentation algorithms: A quantitative assessment, in: International geoscience and remote sensing symposium: remote sensing of the system earth—A Challenge for the 21st Century, IEEE*, pp. 1–3, IEEE Computer Society CD-ROM, Hamburg, Germany.

Gonzalez, R. C., & Woods, R. E. (1992). *Digital image processing*. MA: Addison-Wesley.

Huber, P. J. (1981). *Robust statistics*. New York: Wiley.

Jain, A. K. (1989). *Fundamentals of digital image processing*. Englewood Cliffs, NJ: Prentice-Hall International Editions.

Johnson, N. L., & Kotz, S., & Balakrishnan, N. (1997). *Discrete multivariate distributions*. Hoboken, NJ: Wiley-Interscience.

Kotz, S., Balakrishnan, N., & Johnson, N. L. (2000). *Continuous multivariate distributions: Models and applications* (Vol. 1). New York: Wiley-Interscience.

Lim, J. S. (1989). *Two-dimensional signal and image processing*. Prentice Hall, Englewood Cliffs: Prentice Hall Signal Processing Series.

Lira Chávez, J. (2010). Tratamiento digital de imágenes multiespectrales, 2nd ed., Universidad Nacional Autónoma de México. URLwww.lulu.com.

Mejail, M. E., Jacobo-Berlles, J., Frery, A. C., & Bustos, O. H. (2003). Classification of SAR images using a general and tractable multiplicative model. *International journal of remote sensing, 24*(18), 3565–3582.

Myler, H. R., & Weeks, A. R. (1993). *The pocket handbook of image processing algorithms in C*. EnglewoodCliffs, NJ: Prentice Hall.

Russ, J. C. (1998). *The image processing handbook* (3rd ed.). Boca Raton, FL: CRC Press.

Tuckey, J. (1973). *Exploratory data analysis*. New York: McMillan.

Velho, L., Frery, A. C., & Miranda, J. (2008). *Image processing for computer graphics and vision* (2nd ed.). London: Springer.

Wassermann, L. (2005). *All of statistics: a concise course in statistical inference*. New York: Springer.

Chapter 2
Image Data Formats and Color Representation

The soul becomes dyed with the color of its thoughts.
Marcus Aurelius

2.1 Color Representation

The appearance of an object is basically resulted from: the nature of the light reflected from the object, its optical characteristics, and the human perception. The colors are actually electromagnetic waves described by their wavelength. The visible spectrum, i.e., the portion of the electromagnetic spectrum that can be detected by the human eye, ranges from 390 nm (violet) to 750 nm (red).

There are four main attributes that characterize the light: *intensity*, *radiance*, *luminance*, and *brightness*. In the case of achromatic light, the intensity is the only attribute involved. This is the case where the called *gray-scale* is used: intensity varies from black to white (gray levels in between). On the other hand, in the case of chromatic light, the other three attributes are used to measure the quality of the light source. The radiance refers to the amount of emitted energy by the light source, and it is measured in watts (W). The luminance measures the amount of radiation perceived by an observer, and it is measured in lumens (lm). The brightness is associated to the light intensity. Although the brightness has an accurate interpretation in monochromatic images, it is a very subjective property in the case of chromatic images.

Because of the absorption characteristics of the human eye, the colors are considered to be formed from different combinations of the *primary colors* red, green, and blue. These three colors can be added to create the *secondary colors* magenta (red + blue), cyan (green + blue), and yellow (green + red). The white color can be formed if the three primary colors are mixed or if a secondary color is mixed with its opposite primary color (all in the right intensities).

A. C. Frery and T. Perciano, *Introduction to Image Processing Using R*,
SpringerBriefs in Computer Science, DOI: 10.1007/978-1-4471-4950-7_2,
© Alejandro C. Frery 2013

In color image analysis three attributes are used to differentiate one color from another: *brightness*, *hue* and *saturation*. The hue attribute brings the information concerning the main wavelength in the color, i.e., it is responsible for verifying the color, in the complete spectrum, from red to violet, and magenta. The saturation describes the level of mixture between the hue and the white light, i.e., it defines the "purity" of the color. High values of saturation result in more gray-scale pixels and small values result in pixels with high "purity". For instance, the red color is highly saturated and the pink color is unsaturated. A fully saturated color does not contain white light. Finally, the *chromaticity* is a description that combines hue and saturation. Hence, it is possible to describe an image according to brightness and chromaticity.

The *color depth* measures the amount of color information available to display or print each pixel of a digital image. A high color depth leads to more available colors, and consequently to a more accurate color representation. For example, a pixel with one bit depth has only two possible colors: black and white. A pixel with 8 bits depth has 256 possible values and a pixel with 24 bits depth has more than 16 million of possible values. Usually, the color depths variy between 1 and 64 bits per pixel in digital images.

The *color models* are used to specify colors as points in a coordinate system, creating a specific standard. In the following, the most common color spaces are briefly presented.

2.1.1 RGB Color Model

The RGB (Red, Green, and Blue) color space is one of the most used color spaces, specially for 8 bit digital images. This model is usually used for representing colors in electronic devices as TV and computer monitors, scanners, and digital cameras. The theory of the trichromatic color vision of Young–Helmholtz and the Maxwell's triangle is the basis of the RGB model.

The RGB is an additive model where the red, green, and blue colors are combined on different quantities or portions to reproduce other colors. The pixels of an image represented in the RGB model have usually 8 bits depth, resulting in 256 possible intensities, i.e., the range of [0, 255] for each color.

A color in the RGB model can be described indicating the amount of red, green, and blue. Each color can vary between the minimum value (totally dark) and the maximum value (totally intense). When all the colors have the minimum value, the resulting color is black. On the contrary, when all the colors have the maximum value, the resulting color is white.

This model is known as the RGB color cube, because the model is based on the Cartesian coordinate system and its color subspace of interest is a cube. The primary and secondary colors are at the corners of the cube. The black color is at the origin and the white color is at its opposite corner. The diagonal between the black and the white colors is the gray scale.

2.1.2 CMYK Color Model

The CMYK model is composed by the cyan, magenta, yellow, and black colors. The basis of this model is the light absorption, as the visible colors come from the nonabsorbed light. This space is usually used by printers and photocopiers to reproduce the majority of the colors in the visible spectrum. The system used is called quadrichromie, the subtractive color system, in opposition of the additive system RGB. Cyan is the opposite color of red, i.e., it plays as a filter that absorbs the red color. The same occurs with magenta and green, and with yellow and blue.

Actually, the original subtractive model is CMY. Although equal amounts of cyan, magenta, and yellow produce the black color in theory, this combination in practice (printing on a paper) does not produce a true black. In order to overcome this problem, the fourth color (black) is added to the model (CMYK).

It usually occurs that some visible colors on the screen of a computer monitor are not printed properly on a paper. This happens because the CMYK used in the printers is based on a mixture of inks on the paper, and the CMYK used in the computer monitors is a variation of the RGB space. Consequently, the CMYK color spectrum happens to be smaller than the RGB color spectrum.

2.1.3 HSV Color Model

The HSV color system, created by Alvy Ray Smith, is composed by three components: hue, saturation, and value. This model is also known as HSB (hue, saturation and brightness). These three parameters are used to define the color space as explained before. The possible values for the hue attribute range from 0 to 360 and the values for the other two attributes range from 0 to 100.

The HSV model is based on cylindrical coordinates and it is actually a nonlinear transformation of the RGB system. Hence, it is possible to transform directly a color from the HSV system to the RGB system, and contrariwise (Smith 1978). There are two other color systems related to HSV: the HSL (Luminosity) system and the HSI (intensity) system.

This color system is very interesting, because it allows the separation of the three components of a specific color (hue, saturation, and intensity). It is broadly used in artificial vision systems, as it is a powerful tool for the development of digital image processing algorithms based on the human color perception model. Indeed, the HSV model is well suited to characterize colors in practical terms for human interpretation, differently from the RGB and CMYK models.

In the context of this book, we will make reference to the RGB space only. The details about colors and all the color spaces can be found in Gonzalez and Woods (1991) and Frery and Miranda (2008). The reader is referred to the books by Malacara (2011), Fortner and Meyer (1996) and Fairchild (1997) for further reading.

2.2 Image Formats

There are two main classes of visual information that can be stored in a digital computer: the vector and the raster images. The former are made up by the description of the geometric elements that compose the image using a convenient language. The vector format is ideal to present information that can be described by the junction of simple geometric functions: segments, circumferences, text, and color, for example. In addition, this information can be presented at any scale if necessary. On the other hand, in the case of the raster images, the basic element is a value associated to a position (color recorded to a pixel).

In the following, these two image formats are presented in more detail.

2.2.1 Vector Formats

The core R graphics engine was essentially vector based until version 2.11.0, i.e., the plots were (and still are of course) produced very accurately on vector-based devices. Although guaranteeing the very good quality when dealing with vector formats, the lack of support for rendering raster formats leaded to lower quality outputs. However, newer versions of the R graphics engine already have support to render raster formats leading to better scaling, faster rendering, and smaller files (Murrell 2011), as it will be presented in the next chapter.

Vector formats have the advantage of being superior when the images need to be visualized at many different scales, however, the files produced are usually of greater size, mainly in the case of very complex images. When using vector formats, the original data resolution and form can be maintained and the graphic output is usually more refined and elegant. In the cases where the encoding of topology is necessary and important, vector formats are also a good choice of output, as one can take advantage of more efficient operations that use topological information. However, operations such as spatial analysis and filtering within polygons are impossible.

When it comes to modifying a plot using different softwares, considerations must be made depending on the modifications required. For instance, removing a single shape from the image is only practicable with vector images. However, changing a white background of an image to transparent is only possible using raster images. A final remark about vector formats is its easy conversion to a raster format, so usually it is more manageable to produce a vector graphic and then convert it to raster if some later modifications are needed. Indeed, it is almost impossible to proceed with the other way around.

Some very known and used vector formats include PDF, PostScript, and SVG, which are presented in more details in the following.

2.2.1.1 PDF

Portable Document Format (PDF) is a file format developed by Adobe Systems in 1993 in order to represent documents independently of the application, the hardware or the operational system used to create them (Adobe Systems Inc. 2004). A PDF file can be used to describe documents with text, graphics, and images in a format which is independent of device and resolution.

PDF is an open pattern, which means that everyone can develop softwares to read and write documents in this format. Consequently, there are several available softwares for viewing documents in this format like Adobe Reader, and that is one of the reasons why PDF is a good choice of format. Additionally, it is a very sophisticated format, so it is able to faithfully produce anything that R graphics can do.

2.2.1.2 PostScript

Encapsulated PostScript (EPS) (Adobe Systems Inc. 1999) was developed by Adobe and, besides being a digital image format, it is a language for description of pages. Instead of defining pixels, PostScript is composed by a set of commands which are interpreted by an output device like printers, for instance. This format can be used to store images, raster formats or both of them. As it does not represent pixels directly, it cannot be read using common softwares for image manipulation, they can be only created by them. PostScript is capable to manipulate text and graphics efficiently and with higher quality than raster formats, however it can not store photos.

In order to print documents in this format, the device used must be capable to interpret PostScript. Because of its popularity, EPS is very used as output and by publishing softwares. Vector editing softwares can open files in EPS format; when opened in image editors, EPS documents are rasterized, i.e., they are converted into pixels.

PostScript can be more sophisticated than PDF, however, it does not support some features like semitransparent colors and hyperlinking, for instance. Consequently, differently from PDF, EPS is not able to faithfully produce everything that R graphics can do.

2.2.1.3 SVG

Scalable Vectorial Graphics (SVG) (Ferraiolo 2003) is a XML language to describe bidimensional graphics in a vectorial form statically, dynamically, or animatedly. Differently from other vectorial formats, no company has the ownership of SVG, i.e., it is an open format. However, it does not loose in sophistication if compared with PDF and EPS. SVG was created by the World Wide Web Consortium (W3C), which was responsible for creating other pattern as HTML and XHTML. A work group inside W3C started to develop SVG in 1999, having as reference other patterns as PGML (Adobe) and VML (Microsoft). SVG is supported natively by most modern Web browsers and they support most static graphics produced in R.

2.2.2 Raster Formats

In the context of digital images, an image format is a common manner to organize and store image data. The format defines how the data are arranged and the used compression type or level. Generally speaking, raster graphics or bitmap files (map of bits), contain a representation of a graphic stored as pixels at a fixed resolution. A common example is a digital photo or a scanned image. Some of the most usual raster formats are GIF, JPEG, PNG, TIFF, and BMP. The book of (Murray and Ryper 1994) is an excellent reference for the main graphic formats.

Image formats can be divided into two classes: binary and continuous tone. A binary image has only two tones, while a continuous tone image contains all the gray levels between white and black. Table 2.1 presents some known raster formats divided into the two classes mentioned before.

The formats presented in the following are directly related to the storage and distribution of photos.

2.2.2.1 TIFF

TIFF (*Tagged Image File Format*) is a flexible format that usually stores 8 bits or 16 bits per color (red, green, blue) for a total of 24 or 48 bits, respectively. The extensions used are TIFF or TIF. This format supports several image compression patterns, including JPEG, JPEG-LS and JPEG-2000. There are different common image readers, but not all of them are capable of reading all kinds of TIFF files. Consequently, this format is mostly regarded as a family of formats than as a unique one. The data inside TIFF files can be *lossless compressed* or *lossy compressed*. Some digital cameras can save in TIFF format using the compression algorithm called LZW [Lempel-Ziv-Welch, see Nelson (1989)] for storing data without loss (lossless compression). This format is not broadly supported by Web browsers, but it is broadly accepted as a photo file pattern for printing business. TIFF supports specific color spaces for certain printing devices defining the CMYK by a set of

Table 2.1 Image formats

Binary	Continuous tone
CCITT Group 3	JPEG
CCITT Group 4	JPEG-LS
JBIG (also JBIG1)	JPEG-2000
JBIG2	BMP
TIFF	GIF
	PDF
	PNG
	TIFF

particular printing inks: cyan (C), magenta (M), yellow (Y) and black (K) colors that compose a subtractive color space.

2.2.2.2 JPEG

JPEG (*Joint Photographic Experts Group*) files store data in a format with loss (in major cases). Almost all digital cameras can save images in JPEG format, which supports 8 bits per color for a total of 24 bits, usually producing small files. When the used compression is not so high, the quality of the image is not so much affected, however, JPEG files can suffer from noticeable degradations when edited and saved recurrently. For digital photos that need repetitive edition or when small artifacts are unacceptable, formats without loss besides JPEG should be used for a better storage. This format is also used as the compression algorithm for many PDF files.

2.2.2.3 PNG

The PNG (*Portable Network Graphics*) format was created as a free and open source version of GIF. This format supports true color (16 million of colors) while GIF only supports 256 colors. PNG stands out when an image is formed by large uniformly colored areas. The lossless PNG format is more appropriate for the edition of figures and the lossy formats, as JPEG, are better for final distribution of photos, because JPEG files are smaller than PNG files. Many old Web browsers do not support PNG format, however, all new browsers support most common variations of this format, including transparency in 8 bits.

2.2.2.4 BMP

BMP (*Windows Bitmap*) supports graphic files inside the Microsoft Windows Operational System. Typically, BMP files data are not compressed which results in big size files. The main advantage of this format is it simplicity and broad acceptation.

2.2.2.5 PBM Formats

The PBM (*Portable Bitmap*) (Henderson 1993) format concerns actually in three different image formats for binary images, gray-scale images and color images. These formats are uncompressed and have a common structure. The three formats are:

- PBM (Portable BitMap)—binary images
- PGM (Portable GrayMap)—gray-scale images
- PPM (Portable PixMap)—color images

The original definition of these formats (invented by Jef Poskanzer in the 1980s) had the aim to enable the transmission of images through electronic mail (e-mail), which did not allow file attachment at that time. Hence, the formats PBM, PGM, and PPM represented the content of the images using ASCII characters. This characteristic allowed the insertion of an image inside an e-mail as if it was normal text. However, this usually resulted in large size messages. The format definition was later modified in order to allow also the binary representation.

The PBM format has the following fields (in this order):

- An identifier (magic number): P1 (PBM ASCII), P2 (PGM ASCII), P3 (PPM ASCII), P4 (PBM binary), P5 (PGM binary) or P6 (PPM binary);
- White space
- Image width in pixels
- White space
- Image height in pixels
- For PGM or PPM:

    - Maximum gray-scale value
    - White space

- Values of the pixels corresponding to the total size of the width multiplied by the height for the PBM and PGM formats and three times this number for the PPM format (three bands). The pixels of the image are ordered from top to bottom and from left to right.

When the content is represented in ASCII, the values of the pixels are given in decimal notation and are separated by a white space, a tabulator space or carriage returns. In the binary versions of the formats, the values of the pixels are stored as plain bytes without any separation.

The tools provided by R for reading and writing images in the formats presented are described in the next chapter.

References

Adobe Systems Inc. (1999). *Postscript language reference manual* (3rd ed.). Reading, MA: Addison Wesley.

Adobe Systems Inc. (2004). *PDF reference version 1.6* (5th ed.). Berkeley, CA: Adobe Press.

Fairchild, M. D. (1997). *Color appearance models*. Reading, MA: Addison-Wesley-Longman.

Ferraiolo, D. J. J. (2003). Scalable vector graphics (svg) 1.1 specification. W3C Recommendation. http://www.w3.org/TR/SVG/.

Fortner, B. & Meyer, T. E. (1996). *Number by colors—A guide to using color to understand technical data*. Heidelberg: Springer.

Gonzalez, R. C., & Woods, R. E. (1992). *Digital image processing*. Reading, MA: Addison-Wesley.

Henderson, B. (1993). Netpbm home page. http://netpbm.sourceforge.net/.

Malacara, D. (2011). *Color vision and colorimetry: Theory and applications.* Press monograph, SPIE. http://books.google.com.br/books?id=xDU4YgEACAAJ.

Murray, J. E., & Ryper, W. V. (1994). *Encyclopedia of graphic file formats.* Cambridge: O'Reilly.

Murrell, P. (2011). Raster images in R graphics. *The R Journal, 3*(1), 48–54. http://journal.r-project.org/archive/2011-1/RJournal_2011-1_Murrell.pdf.

Nelson, M. R. (1989). LZW data compression. *Dr Dobbs Journal, 14*(10), 29–36.

Smith, A. R. (1978). Color gamut transform pairs. *SIGGRAPH Computer Graphics, 12*(3), 12–19. http://doi.acm.org/10.1145/965139.807361.

Velho, Z., Frery, A. C. & Miranda, J. (2008). *Image processing for computer graphics and vision* (2nd ed.). London: Springer.

Chapter 3
Reading and Writing Images with R: Generating High Quality Output

> *Either write something worth reading or do something worth writing.*
>
> Benjamin Franklin

We start this chapter explaining what is the core R graphics engine and how it works. A specific package provides the engine, called grDevices, which is available by default along with the standard installation of R and it is already loaded in each R session. This package provides the necessary tools for the output of graphics in different formats and also for defining graphic parameters as resolution, color, size, and fonts.

The usual process inside an R session, when an user is about to start working with an image, can be basically summarized in three steps: reading the input image, processing it, and writing the output image. The reading process will import the image as a data structure that can be manipulated inside an R session. In addition, R must be capable of rendering the imported image, such that its original aspect ratio should be maintained and also that it could be drawn relatively to the coordinate system of an R plot. In the following, the main functions used for graphics input and output are presented, both for the vector and the raster formats presented in the previous chapter.

3.1 Reading Images

3.1.1 Vector Formats

There is one package that provides a function to read vector format images, which is called grImport (Murrell 2009). As explained in the previous chapter, images in vector formats are represented geometrically. Consequently, when a vector image is

A. C. Frery and T. Perciano, *Introduction to Image Processing Using R*, SpringerBriefs in Computer Science, DOI: 10.1007/978-1-4471-4950-7_3,

imported to R it is represented by a set of *paths*, differently from raster images that
are usually represented by matrices of values. A restriction about the package is that
only images in PostScript format can be read. However, there are softwares that can
be used to convert images in other formats as PDF and SVG to PS, like `Inkscape`
for instance (Bah 2011). Listing 3.1 presents a sequence of R functions that can be
used to read a PostScript image.

Listing 3.1 Example of an R code that reads a vector image using the grImport package

```
1  > library(grImport)
2  > PostScriptTrace("Draw.ps")
3  > draw = readPicture("Draw.ps.xml")
4  > grid.picture(draw)
```

Line 1 of Listing 3.1 loads the `grImport` package. The `PostScriptTrace`
function is used in Line 2 to convert the PostScript image, whose file name is passed
as a parameter, into an XML document describing the contents of the image that
will be read into R. The XML document is created with the same name as the
image file, appending the .xml extension, in the same file path. So, in this example,
`Draw.ps.xml`. In line 3, the `ReadPicture` function is used to read the XML
document created previously, which creates a "Picture" object, `draw`. Finally, in
line 4, the `grid.picture` function creates a grid graphical object representing
the image as presented in Fig. 3.1a.

Other functions provided by the `grImport` package deal with the manipulation
of the *paths* of the image. Once the image is imported inside R, the user can deal with
each path separately. Let us start with a simple example, considering our "draw".
This image is composed by five paths: the green strip, the red strip, the black spiral,
the pink star, and the blue "R". The `grid.picture` function can be used to plot
only an interval of the set of paths, as in line 1 of Listing 3.2, where only the star and
the spiral are plotted, as presented in Fig. 3.1b. In order to see each path separately,
the `picturePaths` function can be used as in line 2. The result is presented in
Fig. 3.1e Line 3 presents another option of the `grid.picture` function, which is
to ignore the fill colors of all paths (see Fig. 3.1c).

The advantage of converting the image into an XML file is that the user can change
some attributes of the paths. For instance, let us change the color of all the paths in
the original image and plot again the paths. These operations are presented from line
5 to 10 and the final result is shown in Fig. 3.1d. The reader is invited to explore more
complex manipulations changing attributes as position, rotations, and colors or even
adding other paths directly inside the XML document.

Let us show a last example using the paths of the imported "draw" image. Suppose
that one want to use a different symbol in a common R plot. As a path imported from
a vector image is a symbol described by its geometrical properties, it can be used
easily as any other symbol by R. Take a look at Listing 3.3 and Fig. 3.2.

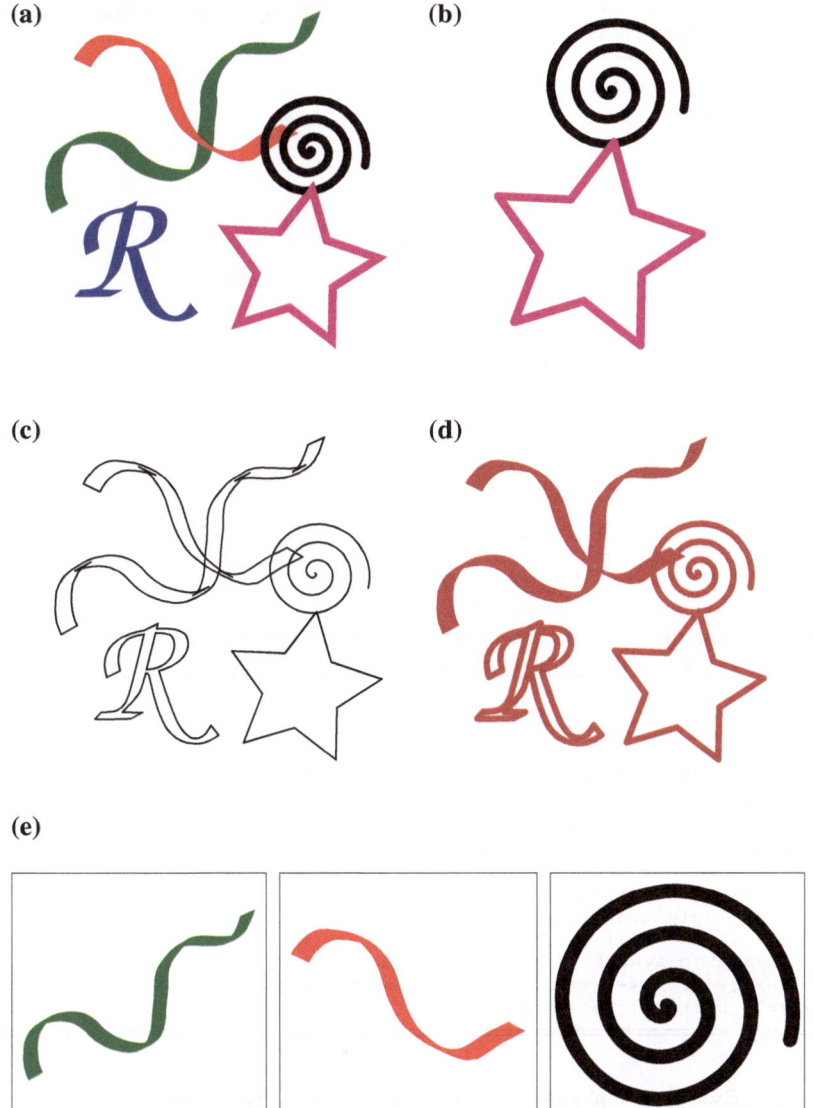

Fig. 3.1 Original vector image imported to R and some results manipulating the paths of the image. **a** Original vector image. **b** Paths 3 and 4 of the original image. **c** Original image plotted ignoring the fill colors. **d** Image after changing the attribute "color" of all the paths. **e** Paths 1, 2, and 3 plotted separately

Line 1 stores all the paths into the variable called paths. In line 2, the spiral symbol is stored into the variable spiral. Lines 3 and 4 create to variables x and y to be ploted. Finally, in line 5, the xyplot is used to plot y against x using spirals

Fig. 3.2 A common R plot
whose points are represented
by *spirals*, the symbol imported from the vector image
"draw"

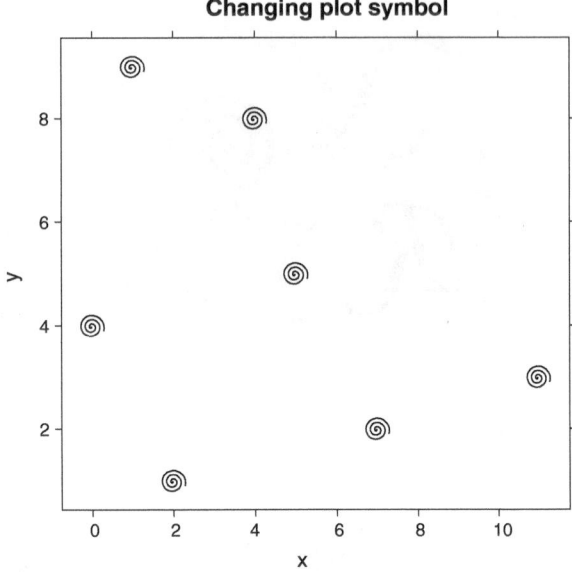

as symbols for the plot. The symbols are defined through the `panel` parameter,
where the `grid.symbols` function is used to set the attributes of the spirals (size
of 7 mm).

Listing 3.2 Example of some functions to manipulate vector images

```
1  > grid.picture(draw[3:4])
2  > picturePaths(draw[1:3],fill="white",freeScales=TRUE, nr=1, nc=3)
3  > grid.picture(draw, use.gc=FALSE)
4  >
5  > drawRGML <- xmlParse("Draw.ps.xml")
6  > xpathApply(drawRGML,"//path//rgb",'xmlAttrs<-',value = c(r = .8,
7  + g = .3, b = .3))
8  > saveXML(drawRGML, "Changeddraw.ps.xml")
9  > changeddraw <- readPicture("Changeddraw.ps.xml")
10 > grid.picture(changeddraw)
```

Listing 3.3 Example of R plot using a symbol imported from a vector image

```
1  > paths <- explodePaths(draw)
2  > spiral <- paths[3]
3  > x = c(1,2,7,4,5,0,11)
4  > y = c(9,1,2,8,5,4,3)
5  > xyplot(y ~ x,main="Changing plot symbol",
6  + panel=function(x,y,...) {
7  + grid.symbols(spiral,x,y,units="native",size=unit(7,"mm"))
8  + })
```

3.1.2 Raster Formats

Some R packages provide useful functions for reading images in raster formats. Six packages and their respective functions will be explored here: pixmap, png, rtiff, ReadImages, EBImage, and bmp. Listing 3.4 presents how to use the ReadImages package, which provides the read.jpeg function. Line 3 loads the library, line 4 reads the image, and Line 5 displays it. Similarly, using the png package, which provides the readPNG function, it is possible to read a PNG image into R as presented in Listing 3.5. In line 3, the package is loaded. In lines 4 and 5 the image is read and displayed, respectively.

Listing 3.4 Code presenting how to read jpeg images into R

```
1  > # Reading jpeg images
2  >
3  > library(ReadImages)
4  > draw <- read.jpeg("Draw.jpg")
5  > plot(draw)
```

Listing 3.5 Code presenting how to read PNG images into R

```
1  > # Reading png images
2  >
3  > library(png)
4  > draw <- readPNG("Draw.png")
5  > plot(imagematrix(draw))
```

In the case of TIFF images, the rtiff package must be used, which provides the readTiff function. Listing 3.6 presents how to use the package (loaded in line 2) in order to read (line 3) and display the image (three channels together as in line 4 or each channel separately as in lines 5, 6, and 7).

Listing 3.6 Code presenting how to read tiff images into R

```
1  > # Reading tiff images
2  > library(rtiff)
3  > draw <- readTiff("Draw.tiff")
4  > plot(draw)
5  > plot(draw@red)
6  > plot(draw@green)
7  > plot(draw@blue)
```

Alternatively to the packages presented before, there is the EBImage package which provides the readImage function that is capable to read JPEG, PNG, and TIFF functions. This package is more sophisticated and provides several functions for manipulating images such as cropping, filtering, and applying mathematical morphology operators. Listing 3.7 presents how to read images in the three formats above using the readImage function.

Listing 3.7 Code presenting how to use the `readImage` function from `EBImage` to read JPG, PNG, and TIFF images

```
1  > library(EBImage)
2  > draw <- readImage("Draw.jpg")
3  > display(draw)
4  > draw <- readImage("Draw.png")
5  > display(draw)
6  > draw <- readImage("Draw.tiff")
7  > display(draw)
```

Finally, Listing 3.8 presents the use of the functions provided by the `bmp` and `pixmap` packages to read BMP and bitmap images respectively. Specifically, lines 2 and 3 show an example of reading and displaying a BMP image. It is important to notice that the `read.bmp` function is limited to 8 bit gray-scale images and 24 bit RGB images. Lines 5 and 6 show how to read and display a PPM image. The `print` function is provided by the `pixmap` package and it presents the general description of the image as presented in line 7

Listing 3.8 Code presenting how to read BMP images into R

```
1  > library(bmp)
2  > draw <- read.bmp("Draw.bmp")
3  > plot(draw)
4  > library(pixmap)
5  > draw <- read.pnm("Draw.ppm")
6  > plot(draw)
7  > print(draw)
8  Pixmap image
9    Type          : pixmapRGB
10   Size          : 222x222
11   Resolution    : 1x1
12   Bounding box  : 0  0  222  222
```

3.2 Writing Images

At the beginning of this chapter we have discussed about the `grDevices` package. This package controls the *devices* where a graphic is going to be displayed. During an active R session, when a graphic function is called, a graphics window is opened. This means that R uses this window as the default device, so the user do not need to decide where to send the graphics output. However, if the user wants to print the graphic in order to use in a document for instance, a graphic device must be specified, so the graphic can be saved in a file. The usual procedure is to call a function that opens a particular graphics device. After this call, all the subsequent outputs of graphic functions are produced on this device. Finally, the device must be closed calling the `dev.off` function. In the following, the different devices available are presented along with specific functions for writing digital images.

3.2.1 Vector Formats

There are three main devices that can be used to save vector images: `postscript`, `pdf`, and `svg`. Let us use the same "draw" from the previous section. Assume that we have read a vector image as presented in Listing 3.1 and we have changed the image as in Listing 3.2. Now, the image can be saved in a specific device as presented in Listing 3.9.

First, the image is plot as default on the graphics window inside the R session (line 1). On the other hand, in line 2, the `postscript` function opens an EPS file and the graphics output of the `grid.picture` function (line 3) is sent to this file. Finally, the file is closed in line 4. The same procedure is carried out using the other two devices as presented in lines 6 to 12. A zoomed region of the saved image is presented in Fig. 3.3b. Observe that the image still has the vector characteristics unchanged if compared with a zoomed region from the original image presented in Fig. 3.3a.

Listing 3.9 R code to save a vector image in a specific file format

```
1  > grid.picture(draw, use.gc=FALSE)
2  > postscript("Draw_postscript.eps")
3  > grid.picture(draw, use.gc=FALSE)
4  > dev.off()
5  >
6  > pdf("Draw_pdf.pdf",width=2.23,height=2.23)
7  > grid.picture(draw, use.gc=FALSE)
8  > dev.off()
9  >
10 > svg("Draw_svg.svg",width=2.5,height=2.5)
11 > grid.picture(draw, use.gc=FALSE)
12 > dev.off()
13 >
```

3.2.2 Raster Formats

In the case of writing in raster formats, the same packages that provide the functions for reading images also provide functions for writing them. In addition, the `writeJPEG` function provided by the `jpeg` package is used. Listing 3.10 presents examples on how to use the functions for each raster format.

In lines 1 and 2 the image is read as learned in the previous section. In line 3, the values of some pixels are changed to 0.3. The changed image is written in JPEG, PNG, and TIFF in lines 5, 8, and 11, respectively. In the case of the TIFF format, the image must be converted to a data structure recognized by the `writeTiff` function, and this is done by the `newPixmapRGB` function. Similarly as the case of reading images, the `EBImage` package can be an alternative option to write in JPEG, PNG, and TIFF formats as presented in lines 15, 16, and 17. Finally, the image is written also in BMP (lines 19 to 21) and PPM (line 24).

Listing 3.10 R code to save images in raster formats

```
 1  > library(ReadImages)
 2  > draw <- read.jpeg("Draw.jpg")
 3  > draw[80:90,85:95,] = 0.3
 4  > library(jpeg)
 5  > writeJPEG(draw,"Draw_jpeg.jpg",quality=100)
 6  >
 7  > library(png)
 8  > writePNG(draw,"Draw_png.png")
 9  >
10  > library(rtiff)
11  > writeTiff(newPixmapRGB(draw[,,1],draw[,,2],draw[,,3]),
12  + "Draw_tiff.tiff")
13  >
14  > library(EBImage)
15  > writeImage(draw,"Draw_jpeg2.jpg",type="jpeg")
16  > writeImage(draw,"Draw_png2.png",type="png")
17  > writeImage(draw,"Draw_tiff2.tiff",type="tiff")
18  >
19  > bmp("Draw_bmp.bmp")
20  > plot(draw)
21  > dev.off()
22  >
23  > library(pixmap)
24  > write.pnm(pixmapRGB(draw),"Draw_pnm.ppm")
```

A zoomed region of the written image in raster format is presented in Fig. 3.3c. The difference between the vector and the raster formats is clear. The quality of the former is visually superior than the latter, as it is described by its geometrical shapes and it is perfectly rendered by R, differently from the raster format.

Fortunately, since version 2.11.0, R have support to render raster formats (Murrell 2011) through the `grid` package. This new support comes to soften the problem when rendering raster graphics, mainly for those that are intrinsically raster, i.e., graphics that are simply composed by an array of values, as the pixels of a digital image. The main advantages of using this new support is the better scaling, faster rendering and smaller graphics files. Listing 3.11 shows an example on how to use the package. In lines 1 to 3, the image is imported and displayed as usual. In line 5, the image is displayed using the `grid.raster` function, which provides the new rendering support. Figure 3.3d presents the resulting image saved using the `grid.raster` function. It can be observed the difference between the images in Figs. 3.3c, d, where the second one is clearly smoother than the first one.

Listing 3.11 Use of the `grid.raster` function

```
1  > library(ReadImages)
2  > draw <- read.jpeg("Draw.jpg")
3  > plot(draw)
4  > library(grid)
5  > grid.raster(draw)
```

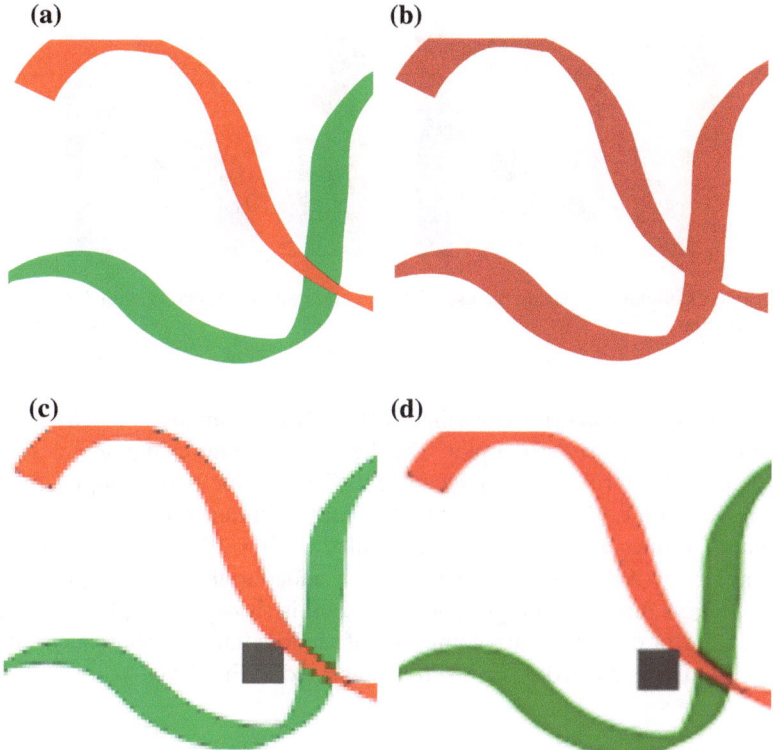

Fig. 3.3 **a** Original image in vector format and different output results. **b** Modified image saved in vector format. **c** Image saved in JPEG format. **d** Image saved in raster format using the `grid.raster` function

The main difference about the `grid.raster` function is that it uses an interpolation process when displaying the image, i.e, instead of displaying the actual pixels (squares of values), it displays an interpolation version of the values. Observe the examples presented in Listing 3.12. Line 2 creates a simple matrix of size 6×8 with 48 different colors. In line 3 the matrix is displayed as usual and in line 4 the same matrix is displayed using interpolation. Both results are presented in Figs. 3.4a, b, respectively.

Listing 3.12 Use of the `grid.raster` function

```
1  > library(grid)
2  > m = matrix(colors()[51:98],nrow=6)
3  > grid.raster(m,interpolate=F)
4  > grid.raster(m,interpolate=T)
```

(a)   **(b)**

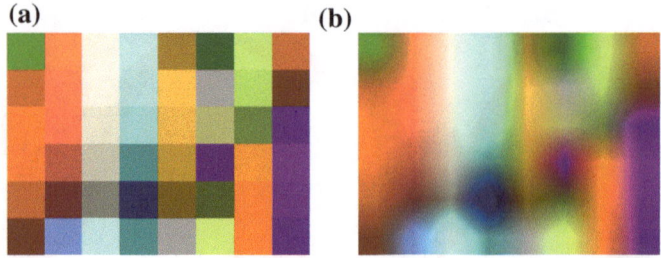

Fig. 3.4 Two examples comparing the use of the `grid.raster` function with 3.4a and without 3.4b interpolation

The `grid` package also provides the `rasterImage` function, which can be used to add a raster image to a usual plot. This becomes an interesting and elegant way to add graphical information to a vector plot. Observe the two examples presented in Listing 3.13. First, a simple $x \times y$ plot is built with the common `plot` function as presented in lines 2 to 4. Then, a matrix of size 30×30 is created with uniform random numbers (line 5). Finally, this matrix is added to the previous plot using the `rasterImage` function (line 6). The final result is shown in Fig. 3.5a. In a second example, a vector of size 50 also composed of random uniform numbers is added to the same plot (lines 8 to 10). The result is presented in Fig. 3.5b.

(a)   **(b)**

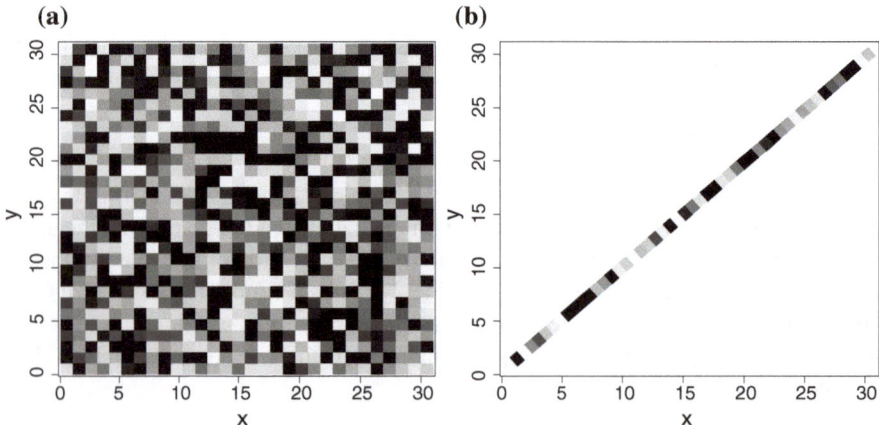

Fig. 3.5 Examples on how the `rasterImage` function can be used to add raster graphics in usual R plots

Listing 3.13 Two examples using the `rasterImage` function

```
1  > library(grid)
2  > x <- 1:30
3  > y <- x
4  > plot(x,y)
5  > image <- matrix(runif(30*30),ncol=30)
6  > rasterImage(image,0,0,31,31,interpolate=F)
7  >
8  > plot(x,y)
9  > z <- runif(50)
10 > rasterImage(z,0,1,1,46,angle=-48.5)
```

More details about input and output in R and image formats can be found in Murrel (2011).

References

Bah, T. (2011). *Inkscape: guide to a vector drawing program* (4th ed.). New York: SourceForge Community Press.

Murrel, P. (2011). *R Graphics* (2nd ed.). Boca Raton: CRC Press.

Murrell, P. (2009). Importing vector graphics: The grImport package for R. *Journal of Statistical Software*, 30(4), 1–37. URL http://www.jstatsoft.org/v30/i04/

Murrell, P. (2011). Raster images in R graphics. *The R Journal*, 3(1), 48–54. http://journal.r-project.org/archive/2011-1/RJournal_2011-1_Murrell.pdf

Chapter 4
Contrast Manipulation

There is a considerable amount of manipulation in the printmaking from the straight photograph to the finished print. If I do my job correctly that should not be visible at all, it should be transparent.

John Sexton

The operations presented in this chapter are comprehended in a set known as *pointwise operations*, which are the most simple operations that can be performed on an image. These operations are defined in a way that each value in the output image depends only on its correspondent value in the input image, i.e., they are characterized for images $f, g : S \to \mathbb{K}$ by operators $\Psi = (\Psi_s)_{s \in S}$ in the form $g = \Psi(f)$ where $g(s) = (\Psi_s(f(s)))_{s \in S}$. In being so, the value of the output image at the coordinate s, denoted by $g(s)$ depends only on the value of the input image at the same coordinate, and $(f(s))$ on the operator defined for it (Ψ_s). The most simple pointwise operator that can be defined is the identity: $\Psi_s(f(s)) = f(s)$ for all $s \in S$. So, $g(s) = f(s)$ for all $s \in S$.

The pointwise operations as defined before are very general, which enables the change of the transformation rule according to the coordinate, i.e., it is possible to define operators $\Psi = (\Psi_s)_{s \in S}$, where $\Psi_s(f(s)) \neq \Psi_t(f(t))$ if $s \neq t$ even if $f(s) = f(t)$. Although this generality is desirable, it is usually sufficient to use the same operations for all the coordinates. In doing so, the pointwise operation is defined by the operator Ψ without specifying it for each element $s \in S$. This kind of transformations is known as *translation invariant*.

Pointwise transformations can be usually specified by visualization tables or Look-Up Tables (LUTs), specially when the range of the images is finite. The images used in this book are in byte format, i.e., $f, g : S \to \mathbb{K} = [0, 255] \subset \mathbb{N}$. For this kind of image, every translation invariant pointwise transformation can be specified and implemented using a LUT of 255 entries or by a vector of 255 entries, where each one of them is a value in $\mathbb{K}$. Consequently, the transformation Ψ is specified by the vector $(v(0), \ldots, v(255))$ using $v(i) = \Psi(i)$ and the transformation is applied

A. C. Frery and T. Perciano, *Introduction to Image Processing Using R*, SpringerBriefs in Computer Science, DOI: 10.1007/978-1-4471-4950-7_4, © Alejandro C. Frery 2013

Fig. 4.1 Example image 1

using $g(s) = v(f(s))$ for each coordinate. In the case of color images the operation is applied for each band of the image, unless we specify another way during the text.

The image shown in Fig. 4.1 will be the example image used for all the operations presented in this chapter.

At first sight the image does not seem to have a good quality. So, before we continue, let us analyze the data of the image to search for some properties in the data that reflect this low quality. Observe Listing 4.1 presented below.

Listing 4.1 Reading the example image 1 and making basic statistical analysis

```
1  > library(ReadImages)
2  > image <- read.jpeg("NatImage2.jpg")
3  > image.data <- data.frame(
4  +   red=as.vector(image[,,1]),
5  +   green=as.vector(image[,,2]),
6  +   blue=as.vector(image[,,3]))
7  > summary(image.data)
8        red                    green                  blue
9   Min.   :0.00000     Min.   :0.00000     Min.   :0.000000
10  1st Qu.:0.01961     1st Qu.:0.01569     1st Qu.:0.007843
11  Median :0.03137     Median :0.02353     Median :0.015686
12  Mean   :0.03608     Mean   :0.02486     Mean   :0.017454
13  3rd Qu.:0.04706     3rd Qu.:0.03137     3rd Qu.:0.027451
14  Max.   :1.00000     Max.   :0.95294     Max.   :0.952941
```

Line 2 in Listing 4.1 reads the image presented in Fig. 4.1. Line 3 transforms each band of the image in a vector, and the three vectors are stored as a dataframe. In doing so, the image is now a collection of observations in $[0, 1]^3$, i.e., without its spatial properties. In line 7, the command summary treats each vector of image.data separately and it returns a description: the minimum and maximum values, the three quantiles: the inferior, the median, the superior and the mean.

The command attach used in line 1 of Listing 4.2 makes the variables in image.data available for use through their names (red, green and blue). Line 2 draws pairs diagram, where each color represents each band of the image as illustrated in Fig. 4.2.

The diagram in Fig. 4.2 shows that the red and green bands are more strongly associated with each other than with the blue band. The graphic also shows that the

Listing 4.2 Statistical analysis of the example image 1 using graphics

```
1  > attach(image.data)
2  > plot(image.data, col=rgb(red, green, blue),
3  > + pch='.')
4  > library(lattice)
5  > cloud(blue ~ red * green, col=rgb(red,green,
6  + blue), pch=19, screen=list(x=-90, y=30))
7  > boxplot(image.data, horizontal=TRUE,
8  + col=c("red", "green", "blue"))
9  > hist(red, probability=TRUE, xlab="Red
10 + band", ylab="Histogram of
11 + proportions", main="")
```

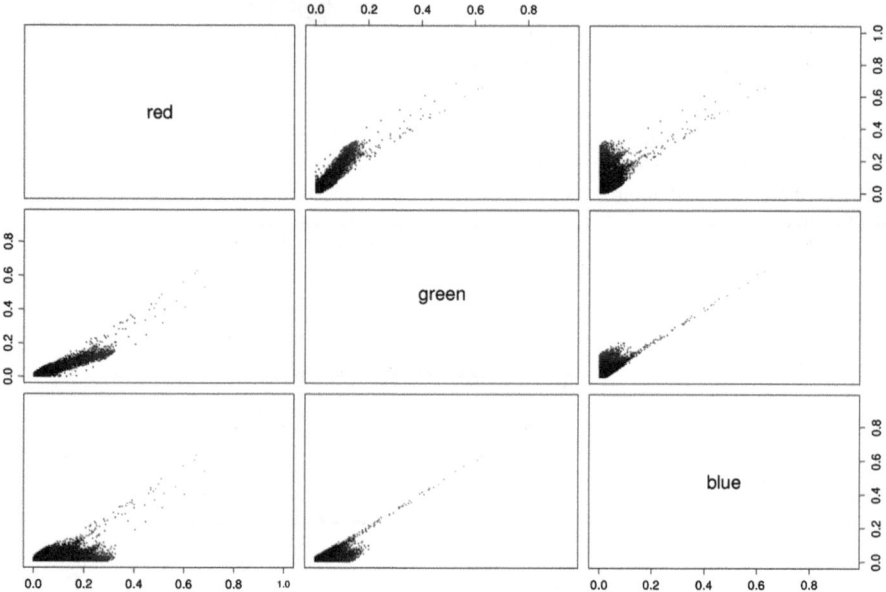

Fig. 4.2 Pairs diagram of the example image showing the correlation between each pair of bands

image has a high quantity of low saturated colors, which are closer to the diagonal that puts together the black and white colors and where the dark shades are predominant.

The simultaneous visualization of the cloud of values in 3D can be created in R using the library lattice, as shown in line 4 of Listing 4.2, along with the function cloud provided by this library (line 5). The created graphic is presented in Fig. 4.3.

In this figure, we notice that a high amount of values are clustered close to the diagonal that goes from the black color to the white color, and consequently, the image had low saturated colors. This effect can attenuate with the techniques of contrast improvement that will be presented later in this chapter. The reader is referred to the books by Jain (1989), Gonzalez and Woods (1992) for more details in contrast

Fig. 4.3 3D perspective of
the values of three bands of
the example image

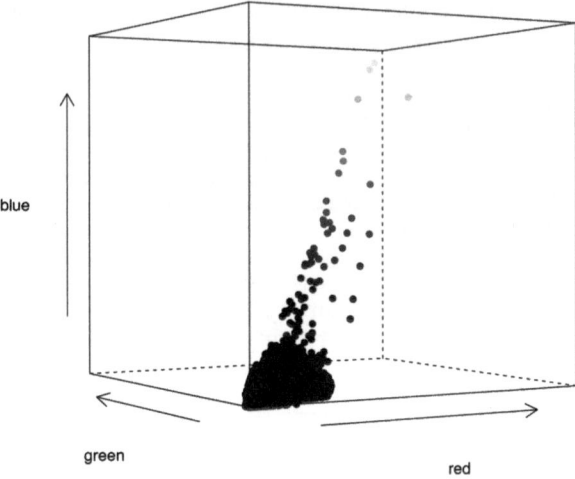

Fig. 4.4 Boxplot of the bands
of the example image, where
it observed the misdistribution
of the values for the three
bands

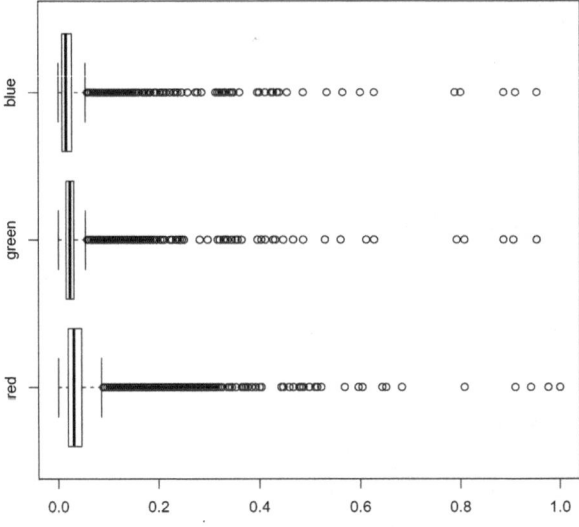

manipulation, and to the books by Murrell (2006), Rizzo (2007) for graphics pro-
duction and statistical computing in R.

Finally, we can build a boxplot and the histogram of each band as shown in lines 7
and 9 of Listing 4.2 (only for the red band). The generated graphics are presented in
Figs. 4.4 and 4.5.

The boxplot reveals that the values for the three bands are not well distributed and
they are more concentrated to the left of the scale (low values), justifying the dark
appearance of the image. These observations can be also seen in the histograms of
the three bands in Fig. 4.5 (left column).

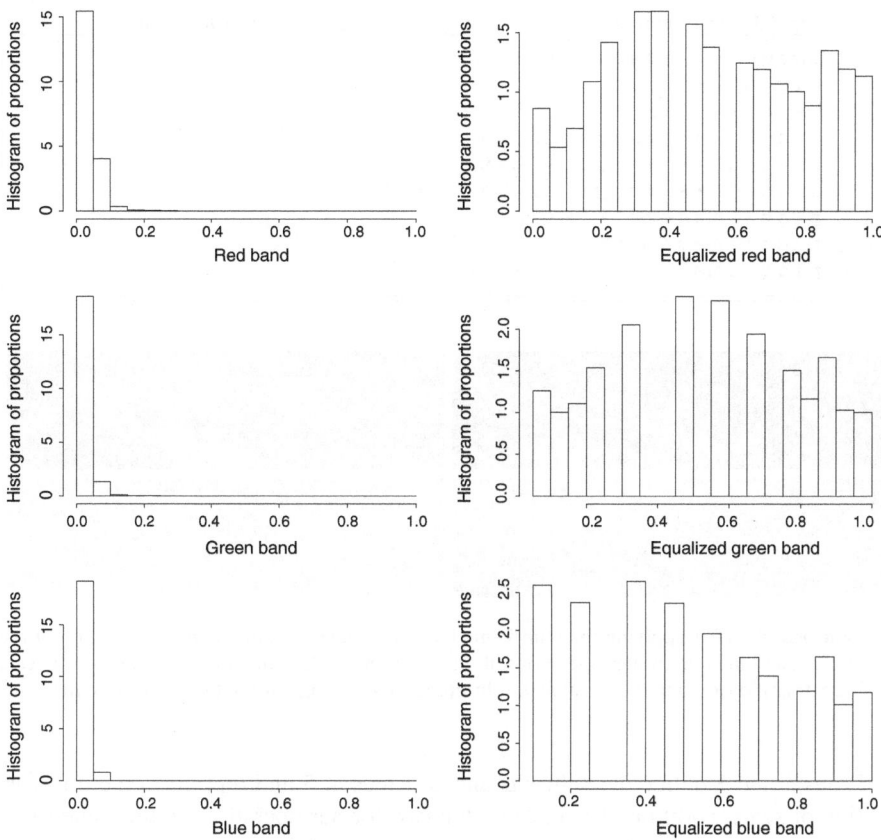

Fig. 4.5 Histogram of the bands of the original image (*left*) and of the equalized image (*right*)

4.1 Brightness and Contrast

For any two real numbers α and β, the pointwise operations "change of scale by α" and "addition of the value β" are defined as $S_\alpha(f) = \alpha f$ and $T_\beta(f) = f + \beta$, respectively, where the former is the product of scalars in each coordinate and the latter is the sum of scalars in each coordinate. The transformation Ψ is "linear" if $\Psi(\alpha f + \beta) = \alpha \Psi(f) + \beta$ for all real numbers α and β and any image f. The linear transformations can be visualized as lines in the space $(f(s), g(s))$. The transformation is "linear by parts" if exists a partition of $\mathbb{K}$ such that for each element of the partition, the transformation is linear. An example of a linear by parts transformation for real images is $g(s) = |f(s)|$.

Listing 4.3 show how to apply the operations of change of scale by α and addition of the value β to the example image 1.

Listing 4.3 Operations of change of scale by α and addition of the value β in R

```
1  > image <- read.jpeg("NatImage2.jpg")
2  > alpha <- 3
3  > beta <- 0.3
4  > image1 <- image*alpha
5  > image2 <- image + beta
6  > image3 <- image*alpha + beta
7  > plot(imagematrix(image1))
8  > plot(imagematrix(image2))
9  > plot(imagematrix(image3))
```

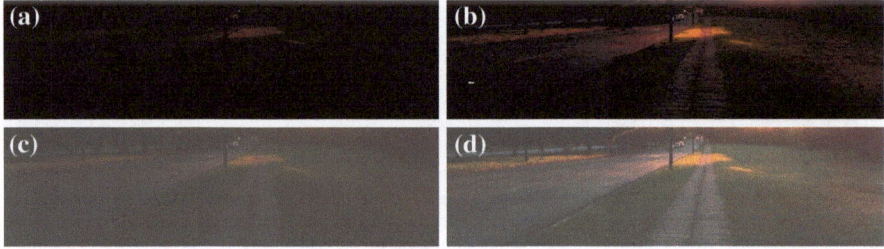

Fig. 4.6 Results after applying the transformations of change of scale by *alpha*, addition of the value *beta*, and the two former operations at the same time. **a** Original image. **b** Change of scale by 3 (contrast). **c** Addition of the value 0.3 (brightness). **d** Change of brightness and contrast

Lines 2 and 3 define the values α and β. Lines 4, 5 and 6 perform the transformation of scale, addition of value, and the two former operations at the same time, respectively. Figure 4.6 shows the result after applying the operations.

As observed in Fig. 4.6, these operations result in brightness and contrast changes in an image where the values α and β are defined by the user. However, it is not always possible to find a pair of values capable to produce an ideal result. Consequently, it is necessary to define a metric to guide the search of these values, as the variance (a contrast measure) or entropy (an information measure).

4.2 Digital Negative

Another simple pointwise operator is the *digital negative*, which can be defined as: $\Psi_s(f(s)) = 255 - f(s)$ for all $s \in S$. Listing 4.4 presents a simple R code that applies this operation on the image of Fig. 4.6d. Line 1 applies the negative operator to the image resulted from line 6 of Listing 4.3 and line 2 plots the result. The values are subtracted from 1 and not from 255 because of the internal conversion applied by the software, so the values are between 0 and 1.

Figure 4.7 presents the result after applying the negative operator.

Listing 4.4 Application of the digital negative operator in R

```
1  > negative <- 1 - image3
2  > plot(imagematrix(negative))
```

Fig. 4.7   Digital negative of an image

4.3 Linear Contrast Stretching

The *contrast stretching* technique, or normalization, is a simple method for contrast improvement that aims to "spread" the histogram of the image, filling the full range of pixel values. The transformation is made by applying a linear scaling function to the image intensities. The normalizing operator applied to an image $f : S \rightarrow \mathbb{K}$ is given by

$$\Psi_s(f(s)) = (f(s) - min_f)\left(\frac{max_{\mathbb{K}} - min_{\mathbb{K}}}{max_f - min_f}\right) + min_{\mathbb{K}}, \qquad (4.1)$$

where min_f and max_f are a lower and an upper bounds of the image, and $min_{\mathbb{K}}$ and $max_{\mathbb{K}}$ are the minimum and maximum values of $\mathbb{K}$.

The values for min_f and max_f could be the actual minimum and maximum values of the input image, however, this could be a problem in the presence of outliers. To overcome this problem these values are usually chosen as the 5th and 95th percentiles of the histogram. In the case of images with more than one band, the operator is applied for each band separately. Listing 4.5 presents the R code used to obtain the normalized image shown in Fig. 4.8.

4.4 Histogram Equalization

The *histogram equalization* is a pointwise operation used to improve the contrast of an image and it belongs to the basic set of image transformations. Unlike the operations shown in the previous sections, the histogram equalization does not depend on the specification of values from the user.

This operation makes use of the intuitive idea that an image with a good gradation of gray levels should have approximately the same amount of positions in each

Fig. 4.8 Result after linear contrast stretch. **a** Original image. **b** Image with stretched histogram

Listing 4.5 Implementing the linear stretching operator and applying it to the example image 1 in R

```
1   > stretch_oper<-function(img,a=0,b=1){
2   >      x <- quantile(img,seq(0,1,by=0.05))
3   >      c <- as.double(x[[2]])
4   >      d <- as.double(x[[20]])
5   >      imgout = (img-c)*((b-a)/(d-c))+a;
6   >      imgout[imgout<a]<-a; imgout[imgout>b]<-b;
7   >      return(imgout)
8   > }
9   > red_stretch <- stretch_opr(red)
10  > green_stretch <- stretch_oper(green)
11  > blue_stretch <- stretch_oper(blue)
12  > stretch <- image
13  > stretch[,,1] <- red_stretch
14  > stretch[,,2] <- green_stretch
15  > stretch[,,3] <- blue_stretch
16  > plot(imagematrix(stretch))
```

possible value of $\mathbb{K}$. In an opposite situation, we would have an image with a unique value, i.e., with no visual information. At first, this image with good gradation of gray levels would have a nearly normal histogram, and events with this type of histogram usually comes from random variables with uniform distribution.

Some elements of statistics defined in the previous chapter are used here to justify the technique of histogram equalization. The Theorem 1.1, for which the proof is presented in Bustos and Frery (1992), gives the theoretical support for the transformation we are looking for. The aim of the desired operation is to obtain the most uniform histogram possible. In order to achieve that, we can model the observed values as events, i.e., as occurrences of the random variable X. As we do not know

Fig. 4.9 Result after histogram equalization. **a** Original image. **b** Equalized image

F_X, the cumulative distribution function that characterizes the distribution of X, we can estimate it. The empirical function (Definition 1.11) can be used in this sense.

The definition 1.11 provides means to estimate F, that according to 1.2 is the transformation that we need to obtain the desired distribution and which was stipulated by definition 1.5. Consequently, we have all the necessary tools to solve the our problem:

1. Calculate the empirical function of the image $f = (x_1, \ldots, x_n)$, that is, to obtain $\widehat{F}(f)$.
2. Obtain the image with the equalized histogram $g : S \to [0, 1]$ by applying pointwise $\widehat{F}$ to f, i.e., $g(s) = \widehat{F}(f(s))$.

When leading with color images, this transformation can be applied independently to each band. As $\widehat{F}$ is just an estimator of F, and because of the discrete nature of the data, the transformed image g will hardly have a perfect distributed histogram. However, the result of the application of this transformation is usually notable, as illustrated in Fig. 4.9. The R code to generate this result is shown in Listing 4.6.

Listing 4.6 Operation of histogram equalization in R

```
> red.eq <- ecdf(red)(red)
> green.eq <- ecdf(green)(green)
> blue.eq <- ecdf(blue)(blue)
> dim(red.eq) <- dim(green.eq) <- dim(blue.eq) <-
+ dim(image)[-3]
> equalized = image
> equalized[,,1] = red.eq
> equalized[,,2] = green.eq
> equalized[,,3] = blue.eq
> plot(equalized)
```

Fig. 4.10 Perspective of values of the equalized example image 1

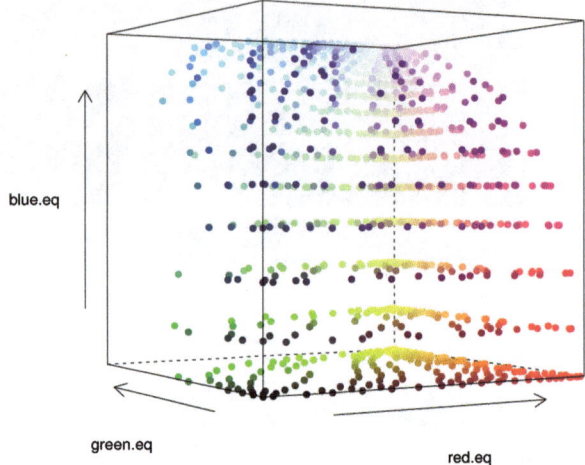

Fig. 4.11 Boxplot of the bands of the equalized image

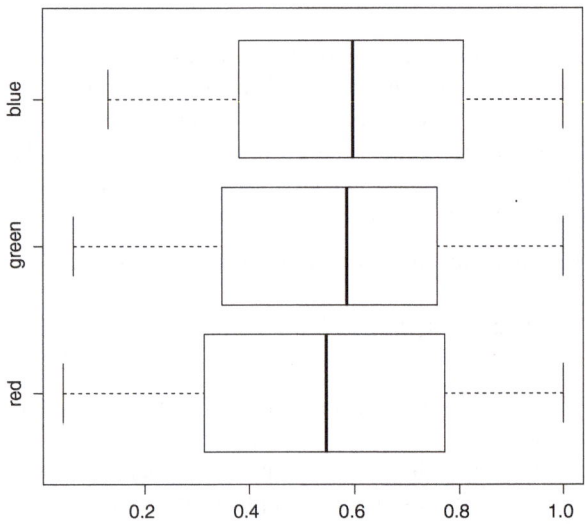

After the equalization process we can remake the same graphics presented in the previous section for the equalized image. Figure 4.10 shows how the values of the equalized image occupy the space. Comparing it with Fig. 4.3, the equalization improves the occupation of the color space and also moves away the colors from the main diagonal of the cube. Similarly, the boxplot of the equalized image shows that the values for each band are more uniformly distributed (see Fig. 4.11). Finally, the histogram of the bands of the equalized images are presented along with the original histograms in Fig. 4.5 (right column).

Theorem 1.1 allows the transformation of any continuous random variable into another random variable with uniform distribution inside the interval (0, 1). Theorem

$$X \sim F_X \xrightarrow{\;F_X\;} U \sim \mathcal{U}_{(0,1)}$$

$$\Big\downarrow F_Y^{-1}$$

$$Y \sim F_Y$$

Fig. 4.12 Diagram of transformation of random variables

Fig. 4.13 Example image 2 with histograms $\beta(5, 5)$

1.2 uses this result to provide an extremely efficient tool for modeling, and it comes to be one of the pillars of the stochastic simulation.

These two theorems can be seen as sets, as presented in the diagram of Fig. 4.12. It is possible, with these theorems, to transform the random variable X that follows the distribution characterized by the cumulative distribution function F_X into the random variable Y that follows the distribution characterized by the cumulative distribution function F_Y using the transformation $Y = F_Y^{-1}(F_X(X))$. This composition of transformations allows us to specify the histogram of an image.

In the following, we illustrate how to specify the histogram with the beta distribution (Definition 1.6). We have already seen this density for different values of the parameters a and b in Fig. 2.2a. We can produce an image with histograms following the density $\beta(5, 5)$. The variables red.eq, green.eq, and blue.eq, which store the equalized bands, will be used as presented in Listing 4.7.

Listing 4.7 Producing an image with histogram specified by the density $\beta(5, 5)$

```
> red.55 <- qbeta(red.eq, 5, 5)
> green.55 <- qbeta(green.eq, 5, 5)
> blue.55 <- qbeta(blue.eq, 5, 5)
> beta55 <- image
> lincol <- dim(image)[-3]
> beta55[,,1] <- matrix(red.55, lincol)
> beta55[,,2] <- matrix(green.55, lincol)
> beta55[,,3] <- matrix(blue.55, lincol)
> plot(beta55)
```

Figure 4.13 shows the result. We can notice the typical effect of a beta density with soft tails and centralized mode: the pastel shades. Using again the visualization in perspective, Fig. 4.14 shows the distribution of values of the image with the specified histogram.

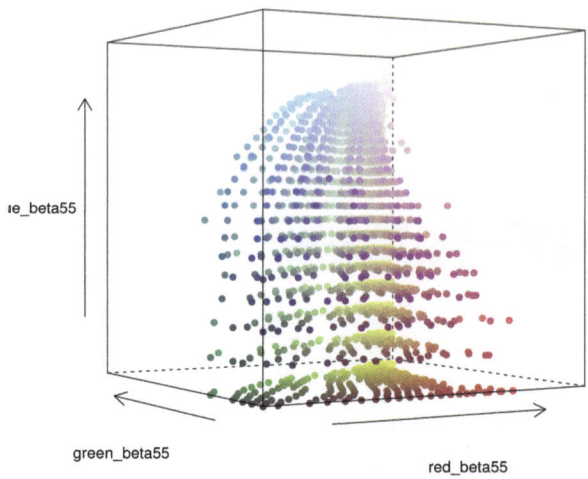

Fig. 4.14 Perspective of values of the example image 1 with histograms $\beta(5, 5)$

Fig. 4.15 Example image 2

The histogram equalization process presented before was applied at one time to the whole image. What if we want to equalize just part of the histogram? This would be the case when we have just one part of the image with dark colors. Let us take a look at the image in Fig. 4.15. Looking carefully to this image, we can notice that there is a clustered set of pixels with high saturated colors. This information can be inferred from the histograms of each band presented in Fig. 4.16 (left column). It

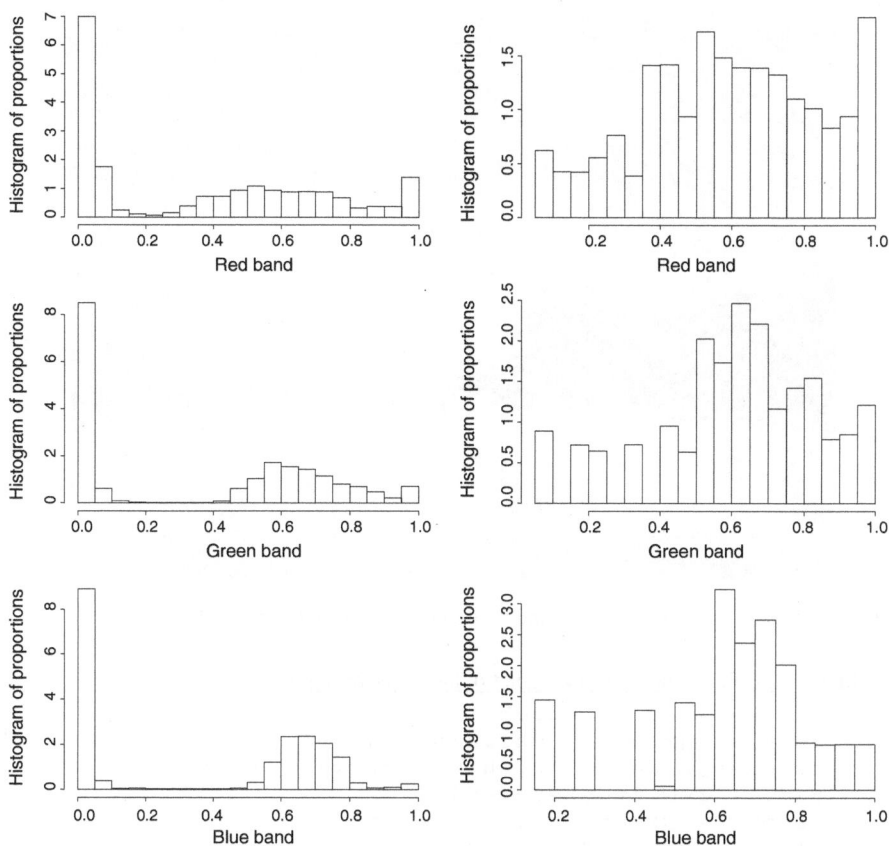

Fig. 4.16 Histogram of the bands of the example image 2 (*left*) and of the adaptive equalized image (*right*)

occurs that each histogram has a division value between the set of low values and high values. Let us try to use this information to apply the equalization technique only to the set of low values. Listing 4.8 shows the R code to make this "adaptive" equalization and the result is presented in Fig. 4.17. The histograms after equalization are presented in Fig. 4.16 (right column).

Lines 1, 2, and 3 use the separation values inferred from the histograms of each band to find only the indexes of the darker pixels using the function which. Lines 4, 5, and 6 take the correspondent values from each band using the indexes found before. As before, we use the empirical cumulative distribution function (ecdf) for the chosen values of each band (lines 7, 8, and 9). Finally, lines 10 to 21 merge the unchanged values and the changed values after equalization, and create the final image shown in Fig. 4.17.

Fig. 4.17 Result of equalizing part of the histogram of the example image 2

Listing 4.8 Experiment equalizing part of the image histogram

```
1  > indexes_red <- which(red<0.22, arr.in=TRUE)
2  > indexes_green <- which(green<0.4, arr.in=TRUE)
3  > indexes_blue <- which(blue<0.45, arr.in=TRUE)
4  > red2 = red[indexes_red]
5  > green2 = green[indexes_green]
6  > blue2 = blue[indexes_blue]
7  > red.eq2 <- ecdf(red2)(red2)
8  > green.eq2 <- ecdf(green2)(green2)
9  > blue.eq2 <- ecdf(blue2)(blue2)
10 > red.eq3 = red
11 > green.eq3 = green
12 > blue.eq3 = blue
13 > red.eq3[indexes_red] = red.eq2
14 > green.eq3[indexes_green] = green.eq2
15 > blue.eq3[indexes_blue] = blue.eq2
16 > dim(red.eq3) <- dim(green.eq3) <- dim(blue.eq3)
17 + <- dim(image)[-3]
18 > equalized2 = image
19 > equalized2[,,1] = red.eq3
20 > equalized2[,,2] = green.eq3
21 > equalized2[,,3] = blue.eq3
22 > plot(imagematrix(equalized2))
```

Using the technique presented is this section, one can specify histograms of different distributions to change the characteristics of an image. The reader is invited to apply this technique using different distributions and different images.

Additional material related to histogram processing can be found in Hummel (1975), Gonzales and Fittes (1977), Stark (2000), Coltuc et al. (2006), Zhu et al. (1999).

In this chapter, some common methods for contrast manipulation were presented. However, there are more advanced and powerfull tools that can be used for contrast enhancement as, for instance, Principal Component Analysis that is presented later in Chap. 6.

References

Bustos, O. H., & Frery, A. C. (1992). *Simulação estocástica: teoria e algoritmos (versão completa), Monografias de Matemática, 49*. Rio de Janeiro, RJ: CNPq/IMPA.

Coltuc, D., Bolon, P. & Chassery, J.-M. (2006). Exact histogram specification. *IEEE Transactions on Image Processing*, 15(5), 1143–1152. http://dblp.uni-trier.de/db/journals/tip/tip15.html#ColtucBC06

Gonzales, R., & Fittes, B. (1977). Gray-level transformations for interactive image enhancement. *Mechanism and Machine Theory*, 12(1), 111–122. URL http://www.sciencedirect.com/science/article/pii/0094114X77900623, Special Issue: Robots and Manipulator Systems.

Gonzalez, R. C., & Woods, R. E. (1992). *Digital Image Processing*. MA: Addison-Wesley.

Hummel, R. A. (1975). Histogram modification techniques. *Computer Graphics and Image Processing*, 4(3), 209–224. URL http://www.sciencedirect.com/science/article/pii/0146664X7590009X

Jain, A. K. (1989). *Fundamentals of Digital Image Processing*. Englewood Cliffs: Prentice-Hall International Editions.

Murrell, P. (2006). *R Graphics*. Boca Raton: Chapman & Hall.

Rizzo, M. L. (2007). *Statistical Computing with R*. Boca Raton: Chapman & Hall/CRC.

Stark, J. A. (2000). Adaptive image contrast enhancement using generalizations of histogram equalization. *IEEE Transactions on Image Processing*, 9, 889–896.

Zhu, H., Chan, F. H. & Lam, F. (1999). Image contrast enhancement by constrained local histogram equalization. *Computer Vision and Image Understanding*, 73(2), 281–290. http://www.sciencedirect.com/science/article/pii/S1077314298907238

Chapter 5
Filters in the Image Domain

> *Filtro de Amor: 20 vellos tuyos, 3 gramos de polvo de tus uñas, o tres gotas de tu sangre (imprescindible; es la clave del filtro de amor, sirve para que el efecto de amor del filtro vaya dirigido hacia ti). http://www.tarot-amor-gratis.com/filtro_amor.htm*

In this chapter we will see how to build filters defined on the image domain. They all share the property of being functions of values around the pixel being processed, so we will not consider approaches based on transformations as, for instance, Fourier or Wavelet domain. Albeit limited, this approach will allow the user to build and experiment with image filters. A more model-based approach can be found in the book by Velho et al. (2008). Other important references are the works by Barrett and Myers (2004); Jain (1989); Lim (1989); Lira Chávez (2010); Gonzalez and Woods (1992); Myler and Weeks (1993); Russ (1998) among many others.

The reader is invited to recall the definitions of *local operations, neighborhood* and *mask* presented in Chap. 1 (p. x and 6). All the filters we consider will be defined on a mask: if f is the input image, then $g = \Upsilon_M(f)$ is the result of applying the filter Υ with respect to the mask M to f. Each element of g is a function of the values observed in f locally with respect to the mask M and the values it conveys. For the sake of simplicity, all considered masks will be of the form presented in Eq. (2.3):

$$M = \left[-\frac{\ell-1}{2}, \frac{\ell+1}{2}\right] \times \left[-\frac{\ell-1}{2}, \frac{\ell+1}{2}\right],$$

i.e., masks are squared sets of coordinates of (odd) side ℓ. Oftentimes, we will need to define values in each mask coordinate, i.e., we will work with matrices of the form $(m_{i,j})_{(\ell-1)/2 \leq i,j \leq (\ell+1)/2}$. The term "mask" and the notation M will be employed for both the support and the values.

For the sake of simplicity, in all the theoretical descriptions we will assume that the input and output images are defined on the infinite support $S = \mathbb{Z}^2$. When implementing the filters, the finite nature of the images needs to be taken into account. This can be done in at least two ways, namely, modifying the mask whenever needed

A. C. Frery and T. Perciano, *Introduction to Image Processing Using R*,
SpringerBriefs in Computer Science, DOI: 10.1007/978-1-4471-4950-7_5,
© Alejandro C. Frery 2013

(close to the edges of the original image), or applying the transformation only to those coordinates where the mask fits in. The latter will be used in our examples, as illustrated in the following code that will be common to all filters here discussed.

Listing 5.1 presents the general convolution filter. It takes two arguments as input, the image to be filtered and the mask. The first operations consist in discovering the number of lines and columns of the original image (lines 6 and 7, respectively), and the side of the mask (line 8). Line 10 creates the container for the output image g by copying the input image f; g is created with the dimensions, type, and additional attributes f has.

Listing 5.1 Convolution filter

```
1   ConvolutionFilter <- function(f, m){
2
3   # f input image
4   # m mask
5
6   llines <- dim(f)[1]
7   columns <- dim(f)[2]
8   k <- dim(m)[1]
9
10  g <- f
11  km1d2 <- (k-1)/2
12
13  for(i in ((k-1)/2+1):(llines-(k-1)/2-1)) {
14    for(j in ((k-1)/2+1):(columns-(k-1)/2-1)) {
15        g[i,j] <- sum( f[(i-km1d2):(i+km1d2),(j-km1d2):(j+km1d2)]
16                       * m )
17      }
18    }
19
20  return(g)
21  }
```

Assume f has m lines and n columns, and that it will be filtered by a mask of (even) side k. If we choose to filter only those pixels over which the mask fits, then our filter must start in line and column $(k - 1)/2 + 1$, and stop in line $m - (k - 1)/2 - 1$ and column $n - (k - 1)/2 - 1$. Listing 5.1 performs this in lines 13 and 14; please notice the use of parenthesis, they are mandatory due to the operations precedence. Lines 15 and 16 are the core of the filtering procedure. The former captures the values in the image which are relevant, i.e., those which correspond to the mask centered at coordinate (i, j). These values retain their matrix nature, and are multiplied, value by value, by the ones in the mask (line 16). Once the product has been performed, the sum command adds all the values.

Notice that Listing 5.1 does not perform any check on the dimensions of either the image f or the mask m. The reader is invited to make this function more robust by verifying, for instance, that the side of m is odd and that there are enough coordinates in f with respect to the size of m for the filter to be applied.

Figure 5.1a presents the image we will use to illustrate the results of applying filters. It is a 320×403 pixels scanned image of an *ex libris* in shades of gray. A line 80 has been drawn in black, and the values are plotted in Fig. 5.1b; notice how

Fig. 5.1 **a** Original image and selected line. **b** Values at line 240 original image, selected line, and values at line 80

(a)

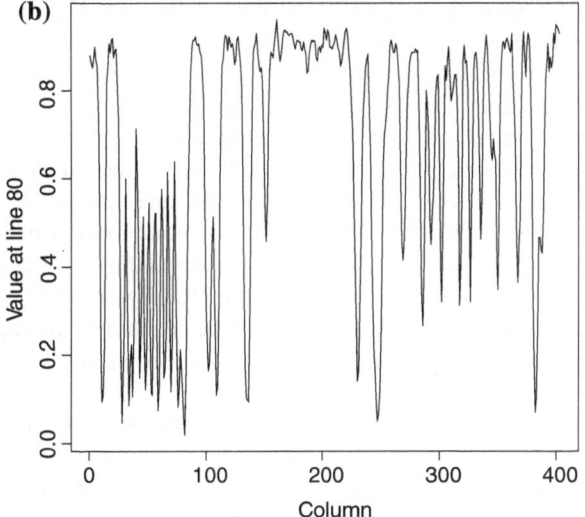

(b)

bright areas intersected by this strip appear as values close to 1, whereas dark regions correspond to values close to 0.

It is noteworthy how some image features translate into profile variation. See, for instance, the tightly packed vertical dark strips which cross the profile to the left in Fig. 5.1a. They appear as a rapidly varying signal in Fig. 5.1b. This will be one of the most affected features due to its relatively small size and high contrast. The high values around column 200 correspond to the light region below the "O", with small variations due to noise.

The following sections will deal with two of the main types of filters that can be defined on the data domain: convolutional and order statistics.

5.1 Convolutional Filters

Listing 5.1 presents the general structure of a convolutional filter. Any convolutional filter is defined by means of the values of the mask $m = (m_{ij})_{(\ell-1)/2 \leq i, j \leq (\ell+1)/2}$, with ℓ the (odd) side of the mask, provided these values are held constant regardless the coordinate they are applied to and the values of the input image f. We say that $g = f * m$ is the result of applying to f the convolution filter defined by the mask m when the output image is defined by

$$g(i, j) = \sum_{-\frac{\ell-1}{2} \leq \imath', \jmath' \leq \frac{\ell-1}{2}} f(i - \imath', j - \jmath') \, m(\imath', \jmath'), \qquad (5.1)$$

for every (i, j). This operation consists in overlaying the mask on each coordinate of f, making the product of each value in the mask with the corresponding value in the image, and then adding all the products to compute the corresponding value in the output image g. R performs this in a rather economic way; in fact, `f[(i-km1d2):(i+km1d2),(j-km1d2):(j+km1d2)]` (line 15 of Listing 5.1) captures all the required values in the input image f. Then `* m` (line 16) performs the pointwise product of these values with those in the mask m. Finally, the command `sum` returns the sum of all these products.

The result will depend only on the definition of the values in the mask. There are many ways to specify masks depending on the desired output. The reader is referred to the book by Goudail and Réfrégier (2003) for a comprehensive account of approaches. Particular masks will be denoted by the capital letter M with a mnemonic subscript. The identity mask $M_\mathbb{1}$, defined as $m_{00} = 1$ and zero elsewhere, produces a copy of f, i.e., $f = f * M_\mathbb{1}$.

If all the entries of the mask are nonnegative, the filter is usually called "low-pass" because, when analyzed in the frequency domain, any filter of this class will reduce the high-frequency content (mainly due to noise and abrupt changes as, for instance, edges and small features) enhancing the low-frequency component (which is associated to flat or slowly varying areas). The books by Jain (1989) and Lim (1989) are excellent references for the analysis of images in the frequency domain, of which we will only borrow some terminology. In the following we will see the effect of a number of low-pass filters.

The first class of low-pass filters we will analyze is formed by those which consist of computing the mean using a some or all the elements of the mask. Consider the following masks:

$$M_5 = \begin{pmatrix} 0 & 1/5 & 0 \\ 1/5 & 1/5 & 1/5 \\ 0 & 1/5 & 0 \end{pmatrix},$$

$$M_9 = \begin{pmatrix} 1/9 & 1/9 & 1/9 \\ 1/9 & 1/9 & 1/9 \\ 1/9 & 1/9 & 1/9 \end{pmatrix}, \quad M_{13} = \begin{pmatrix} 0 & 0 & 1/13 & 0 & 0 \\ 0 & 1/13 & 1/13 & 1/13 & 0 \\ 1/13 & 1/13 & 1/13 & 1/13 & 1/13 \\ 0 & 1/13 & 1/13 & 1/13 & 0 \\ 0 & 0 & 1/13 & 0 & 0 \end{pmatrix}, \quad (5.2)$$

$$M_{121} = (1/121) \text{ in every } -5 \leq i, j \leq 5. \tag{5.3}$$

They all add up to 1, a very convenient normalization in light of the following result.

Claim (The mean value of images filtered by convolution) Let f be an image such that its mean value is finite, and m a finite mask conveying finite values. The mean value of $g = f * m$ is the product of the mean values of f and of m.

Since more often than not we will be working with images defined on a compact set of values K, the unitary cube $[0, 1]^3$ for instance, this result allows us to transform f into g, whose values are not too far from K.

Listing 5.2 shows how to create the masks and the use of the ConvolutionFilter function already defined in Listing 5.1.

Listing 5.2 Building masks and applying mean filters

```
> (m5 <- matrix(c(0,.2,0,.2,.2,.2,0,.2,0), nrow=3))
     [,1] [,2] [,3]
[1,]  0.0  0.2  0.0
[2,]  0.2  0.2  0.2
[3,]  0.0  0.2  0.0
> m9 <- matrix(replicate(9, 1/9), nrows=3)
> m13 <- matrix(c(0,0,1,0,0,0,1,1,1,0,1,1,1,1,1,
+ 0,1,1,1,0,0,1,0,0)/13, nrow=5)
> m121 <- matrix(replicate(n=25, 1/121), nrow=5)

g5 <- ConvolutionFilter(Stanford, m5)
```

Figure 5.2 shows the result of applying the masks defined in Eqs. (5.2) and (5.3) The blurring effect in the first three is subtle, and becomes evident in the last one.

Figure 5.3 shows the profile of the original and filtered images restricted to the vertical strips. Notice the smoothing effect which consists in reducing the width of the peak, up to the point of almost eliminating the variability when the M_{121} mask is applied. The mean value, as expected, is preserved. Notice also that the characters become almost solid, but heavily blurred. The untouched region close to the edges is noticeable in this last example.

(a)   **(b)**

(c)   **(d)**

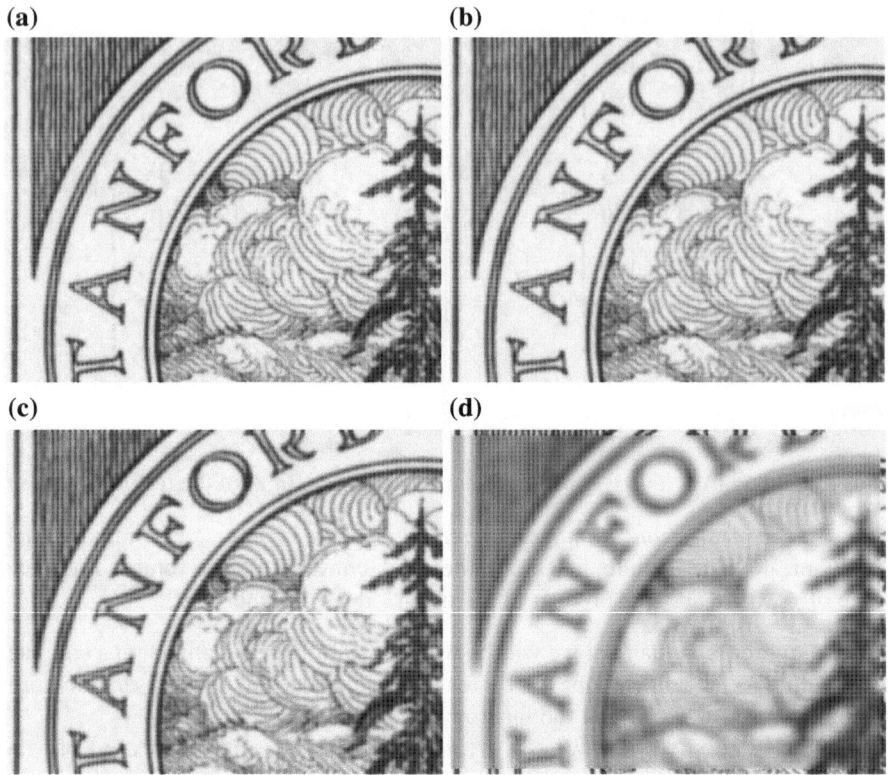

Fig. 5.2 Results of applying mean filters to the original image. **a** $f * M_5$. **b** $f * M_9$. **c** $f * M_{13}$. **d** $f * M_{121}$

Convolution is quite general and is not limited to equal values, as considered so far. Besides the mean filter, another important low-pass convolution filter is the Gaussian mask. A Gaussian mask of side ℓ and standard deviation σ is defined by first computing

$$m'(i, j) = \exp\left\{ -\frac{1}{2\sigma^2}(i^2 + j^2) \right\}, \tag{5.4}$$

for $-(\ell - 1)/2 \leq i, j \leq (\ell - 1)/2$ and then using the normalized mask $m = m' / \sum m(i, j)$. These values decrease exponentially fast from the center to the edges of the mask. Gaussian convolution filters are at the core of multilevel techniques (Medeiros et al. 2010).

Listing 5.3 presents the code that returns the Gaussian mask of side side and standard deviation s. Lines 3–5 define the auxiliary function DExp; it was defined within the scope of GaussianMask in order to make it aware of the input parameter s since, as required later, it has to have as arguments the two variables that will comprise the grid. This auxiliary function implements Eq. (5.4).

Fig. 5.3 Strips profiles at line 240

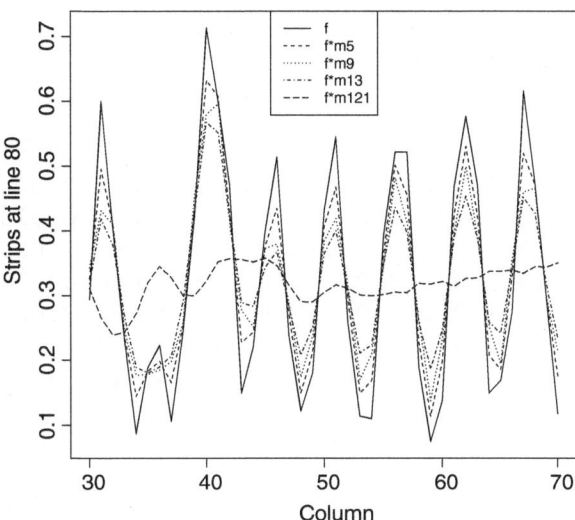

Listing 5.3 Building a Gaussian mask

```
1  GaussianMask <- function(side, s) {
2
3    DExp <- function(x,y) {
4      exp(-(x^2+y^2)/(2*s^2))
5    }
6
7    x <- (-(side-1)/2):((side-1)/2)
8    mask <- outer(x, x, FUN="DExp")
9    mask <- mask / sum(mask)
10   return(mask)
11 }
```

Line 7 builds one of the variables that will define the support of the mask, say i. There is no need to build the other variable (j) since they are equal: $-(\ell-1)/2 \leq i$, $j \leq (\ell-1)/2$. The function outer used in line 8 takes as input two vectors (the same in our case) and returns a grid whose values are the result of instantiating the function DExp in each of all the possible pairs of values of the input vectors. Line 9 normalizes the result in order to make the sum one.

The following code illustrates three examples of Gaussian masks as computed by the function presented in Listing 5.3, all of them of side five with varying standard deviations. Notice that when $\sigma \to 0$ the Gaussian mask converges to the identity mask, while when $\sigma \to \infty$ it becomes the mean over all the elements of the mask.

```
> (GaussianMask(5,.5))
         [,1]     [,2]     [,3]     [,4]      [,5]
[1,] 7.0e-08 2.8e-05 0.00021 2.8e-05  7.0e-08
[2,] 2.8e-05 1.1e-02 0.08373 1.1e-02  2.8e-05
```

```
[3,] 2.1e-04 8.4e-02 0.61869 8.4e-02 2.1e-04
[4,] 2.8e-05 1.1e-02 0.08373 1.1e-02 2.8e-05
[5,] 7.0e-08 2.8e-05 0.00021 2.8e-05 7.0e-08
> (GaussianMask(5,1))
        [,1]   [,2]   [,3]   [,4]   [,5]
[1,] 0.003 0.013 0.022 0.013 0.003
[2,] 0.013 0.060 0.098 0.060 0.013
[3,] 0.022 0.098 0.162 0.098 0.022
[4,] 0.013 0.060 0.098 0.060 0.013
[5,] 0.003 0.013 0.022 0.013 0.003
> (GaussianMask(5,10))
        [,1]   [,2]   [,3]   [,4]   [,5]
[1,] 0.039 0.040 0.040 0.040 0.039
[2,] 0.040 0.040 0.041 0.040 0.040
[3,] 0.040 0.041 0.041 0.041 0.040
[4,] 0.040 0.040 0.041 0.040 0.040
[5,] 0.039 0.040 0.040 0.040 0.039
```

Figure 5.4 shows the result of applying two Gaussian filters with the same window ($\ell = 5$) and two different values of standard variation: Figure 5.4a is the result for $\sigma = 1$, while Fig. 5.4b is the result for $\sigma = 10$. The difference is noticeable: the latter is more blurred than the former.

Somewhere between the mean filters, which has binary coefficients, and the Gaussian filter, whose values decay exponentially with the Euclidean distance to the center of the mask, there is the binomial filter. The binomial mask is defined as the product of all the binomial coefficients $C_i^\ell = \ell!/(i!(\ell - i)!)$, where ℓ is even (so the vector and the mask are odd) and $0 \leq i \leq \ell$.

The code presented in Listing 5.4 shows how to compute this masks in R using the choose function, the product of vectors (and matrices) \%*\%, and the transpose

(a)   **(b)**

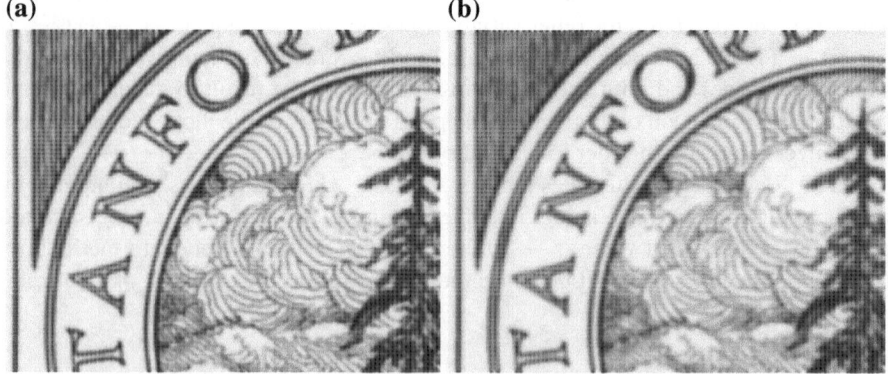

Fig. 5.4 Results of applying the Gaussian filter of side $\ell = 5$ and varying σ. **a** $\sigma = 1$. **b** $\sigma = 10$

operator t. The values are shown before dividing by the sum of the mask, but the operation commented in line 4 must be activated when building binomial masks.

Listing 5.4 Building a binomial mask

```
1   BinomialMask <- function(ell) {
2
3       mask <- choose(ell, 0:ell) %*% t(choose(ell, 0:ell))
4       % return(mask/sum(mask))
5   }
```

A few binomial masks are shown in the following.

```
> BinomialMask(4)
      [,1] [,2] [,3] [,4] [,5]
[1,]    1    4    6    4    1
[2,]    4   16   24   16    4
[3,]    6   24   36   24    6
[4,]    4   16   24   16    4
[5,]    1    4    6    4    1
> BinomialMask(6)
      [,1] [,2] [,3] [,4] [,5] [,6] [,7]
[1,]    1    6   15   20   15    6    1
[2,]    6   36   90  120   90   36    6
[3,]   15   90  225  300  225   90   15
[4,]   20  120  300  400  300  120   20
[5,]   15   90  225  300  225   90   15
[6,]    6   36   90  120   90   36    6
[7,]    1    6   15   20   15    6    1
> BinomialMask(8)
      [,1] [,2] [,3] [,4] [,5] [,6] [,7] [,8] [,9]
[1,]    1    8   28   56   70   56   28    8    1
[2,]    8   64  224  448  560  448  224   64    8
[3,]   28  224  784 1568 1960 1568  784  224   28
[4,]   56  448 1568 3136 3920 3136 1568  448   56
[5,]   70  560 1960 3920 4900 3920 1960  560   70
[6,]   56  448 1568 3136 3920 3136 1568  448   56
[7,]   28  224  784 1568 1960 1568  784  224   28
[8,]    8   64  224  448  560  448  224   64    8
[9,]    1    8   28   56   70   56   28    8    1
```

Figure 5.5 presents the results of applying the binomial masks of sides 7 and 13 to the input image. Notice that the contrast is reduced in the second with respect to the first due to the extent of the mask; it "mixes" the values and both pure black and white tend to disappear.

(a)   **(b)**

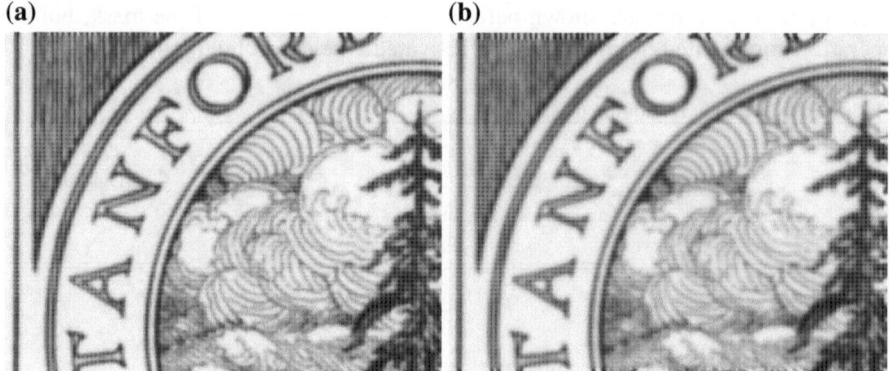

Fig. 5.5 Result of applying the binomial masks. **a** Binomial filter of side 7. **b** Binomial filter of side 13

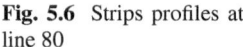

Fig. 5.6 Strips profiles at line 80

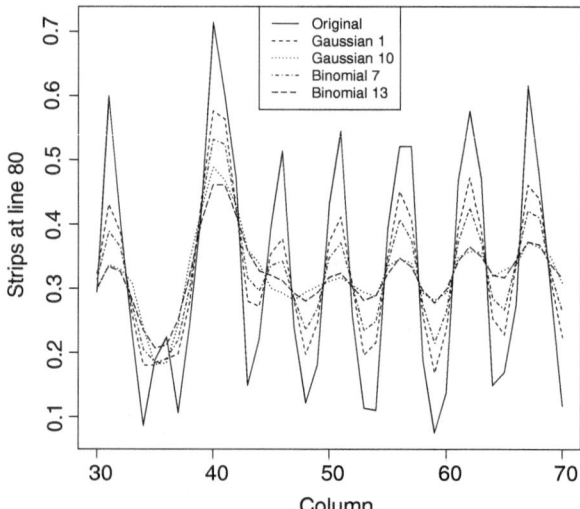

Figure 5.6 presents the profile of line 80 at the strips (columns 30–70) of the original image, and of the images filtered by the Gaussian (with $\sigma = 1$ and $\sigma = 10$) and by the Binomial (of sides 7 and 13) masks.

So far we have seen low-pass filters, i.e., those defined by nonnegative values of the filter mask. In the following we will see an important application of high-pass filters, namely edge detection. This will require the use of negative values.

The first class of high-pass filters we will describe is known as *unsharp masking*. The idea is to enhance the rapid variations in the image, which correspond to edges and sharp transitions, by subtracting a fraction α, $0 < \alpha < 1$, of a smoothed version $\Upsilon(f)$ of the original image to the original image f. The result is $|(1 - \alpha)f + \alpha\Upsilon(f)|$, conveniently scaled to the [0, 1] range.

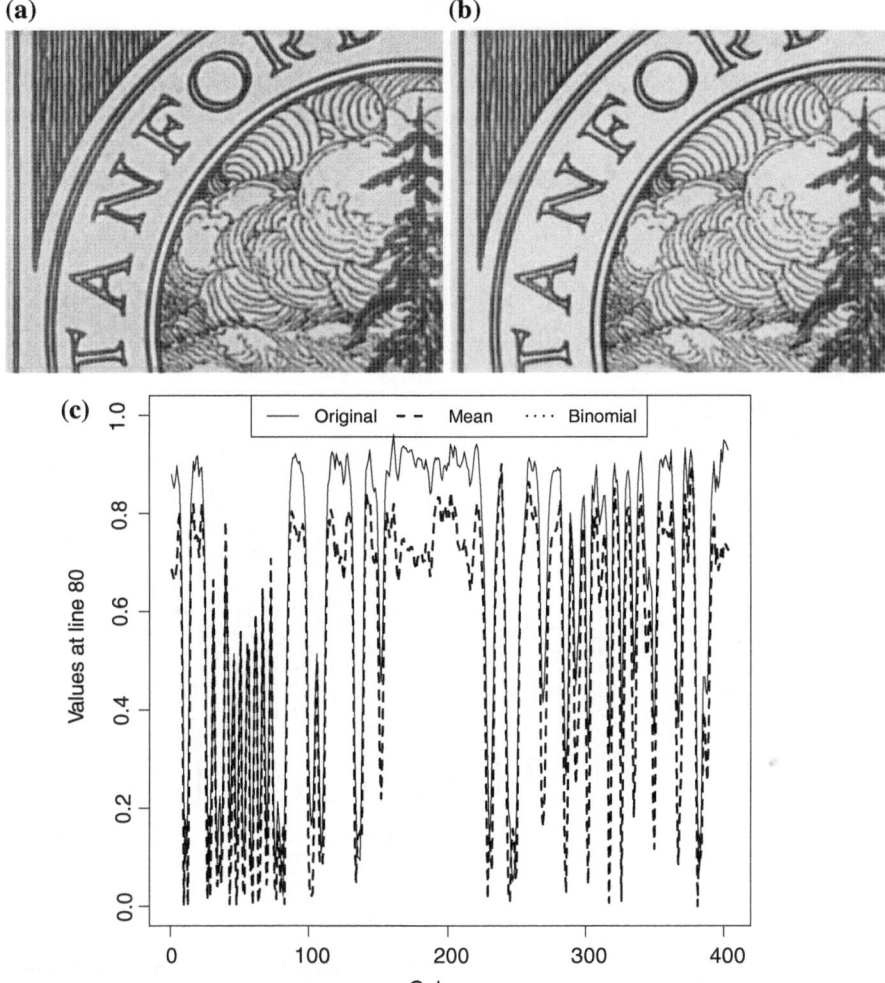

Fig. 5.7 Edge enhancement by unsharp masking with $\alpha = 3/10$. **a** Mean with the M_{121} mask. **b** Binomial filter of side 17. **c** Profiles at line 80

Figure 5.7 presents the results of applying the unsharp masking technique with two different blurred images and the same value of $\alpha = 3/10$. Figure 5.7a was obtained applying the mask defined in Eq. (5.3), i.e., a 11×11 mask of ones, while Fig. 5.7b shows the result of applying the binomial mask of side 17. Albeit the difference between the masks, the results are alike. This powerful technique requires trial-and-error until the desired result is obtained.

Figure 5.7c shows the profile of the original and transformed images. Notice how relatively flat (smooth) areas had their values reduced, while sharp transitions are left unaltered. This transformation leads to a perceptual edge enhancement.

(a)   **(b)**

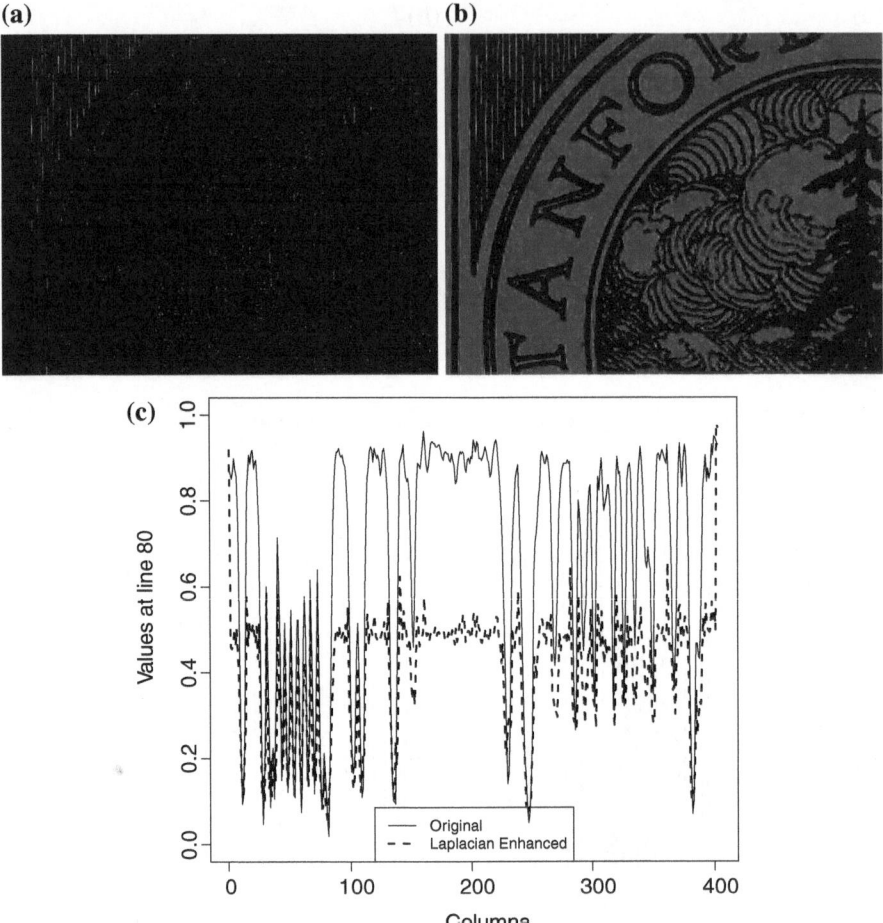

Fig. 5.8 Using the Laplacian mask. **a** Image filtered with the Laplacian mask. **b** Image enhanced with the Laplacian mask. **c** Profiles at line 80

As previously said, oftentimes it is desirable to enhance edges and sharp transitions. If we envision the image $f : S \rightarrow \mathbb{R}$ as the discrete version of a continuous function $\widetilde{f} : \mathbb{R}^2 \rightarrow \mathbb{R}$. Those features could be detected in $\widetilde{f}$ by applying the gradient operator $\nabla = (\partial/\partial x, \partial/\partial y)$, but since we do not possess the analytic (functional) description of $\widetilde{f}$, a discrete version of ∇ could be applied to f instead. This can be performed by convolving the original image with the Laplacian mask:

$$M_L = \begin{pmatrix} 0 & -1 & 0 \\ -1 & 4 & -1 \\ 0 & -1 & 0 \end{pmatrix}. \tag{5.5}$$

The edges detected by the Laplacian mask are shown in Fig. 5.8a. They can be used to enhance the original image by adding the filtered version to it. Replacing the value 4 by 5 in Eq. (5.5) does the trick, and produces the image shown in Fig. 5.8b. Figure 5.8c presents the profiles of the original and enhanced images at line 80. We notice the same effect already described in the unsharp masking technique: a reduction of smoothly varying areas. The Laplacian filter tends to produce noisy images, since it enhances every little variation, even those due to noise.

5.2 Filters Based on Order Statistics

Order statistics can be used in a number of ways to define filters. If $X_1, \ldots, X_n$ is a sample of size $n \geq 2$ from the joint distribution characterized by the density $h^*_{X_1, \ldots, X_n}(x_1, \ldots, x_n)$, then the ordered sample is the vector $X = (X_{1:n}, \ldots, X_{n:n})$ such that $X_{1:n} \leq \cdots \leq X_{n:n}$. A frequent, albeit seldom verified in practice, assumption is that the random variables are independent and identically distributed, so their joint distribution is the product of the marginal one $h^*_{X_1, \ldots, X_n}(x_1, \ldots, x_n) = \prod_{i=1}^n h(x_i)$. Assume also that the random variables are continuous, so the distribution of each is also characterized by the cumulative distribution function $H(x) = \int_{-\infty}^x h(t)dt$, then the following results hold:

- The joint distribution of the ordered sample is characterized by the joint density $h^*_X(x_1, \ldots, x_n) = n! \prod_{i=1}^n h(x_i) \mathbb{1}_{x_1 \leq \cdots \leq x_n}(x_1, \ldots, x_n)$.
- The joint distribution of any pair of ordered samples $(X_{j:n}, X_{k:n})$, $j < k$, is characterized by the joint density

$$h^*_{X_{j:n}, X_{k:n}}(x_j, x_k) = \frac{n!}{(j-1)!(k-1-j)!(n-k)!} h(x_j) h(x_k) \cdot$$
$$H^{j-1}(x_j)(H(x_k) - H(x_j))^{k-1-j}(1 - H(x_k))^{n-k} \mathbb{1}_{(-\infty, x_k)}(x_j).$$

- The distribution of the kth sample is characterized by the density

$$h_{X_{k:n}}(x) = \frac{n!}{(k-1)!(n-k)!} h(x) H^{k-1}(x)(1 - H(x))^{n-k}.$$

The main idea behind using order statistics is that, if well designed, they may lead to robust techniques. By "robust" we mean procedures which behave well if the underlying hypothesis are verified, but that also produce sensible results if they are not true for the data at hand. The reader is referred to the books by Huber (1981) and by Maronna et al. (2006) for a comprehensive introduction to the statistical theory of robustness.

One of the first "robust" approaches to image filtering consists in replacing the mean by the median. This can be easily done modifying the code which implements the convolution filter; cf. Listing 5.1, p. xx.

Listing 5.5 Convolution filter

```
1   MedianFilter <- function(f, k){
2
3   # f input image
4   # k side of the mask
5
6   llines <- dim(f)[1]
7   columns <- dim(f)[2]
8
9   g <- f
10  km1d2 <- (k-1)/2
11
12  for(i in ((k-1)/2+1):(llines-(k-1)/2-1)) {
13    for(j in ((k-1)/2+1):(columns-(k-1)/2-1)) {
14        g[i,j] <- median(as.vector(
15                  f[(i-km1d2):(i+km1d2),(j-km1d2):(j+km1d2)]))
16      }
17    }
18
19  return(g)
20  }
```

The only relevant difference between Listing 5.1 and the median filter presented in Listing 5.5 is in line 14 of the latter. First, the data from the image, which retain their matrix nature, are converted into a vector in order to be able to appy the `median` function. Then the median is computed and stored.

Figure 5.9 presents the result of applying median filters. Figure 5.9a shows the image filtered by the median on 3×3 windows, i.e., using nine observations, while Fig. 5.9b shows the result of using windows of side 11×11, i.e. 121 observations.

The difference between the mean and the median is clear when comparing Figs. 5.2d (p. xx) and 5.9a. The information in the former is almost gone, while it is quite well preserved in the latter (in particular, compare the dark pine tree to the right of the image). This is due to the fact that the mean does not spread the values as intensely as the mean, as can be assessed by comparing Figs. 5.3 (p. xx) and 5.9c. The price one pays for this is that the median is not as effective as the mean at reducing noise.

The reader is invited to write the code that implements the convex combination of the mean and the median filter, i.e., assume $0 \leq \alpha \leq 1$ and a mask of side k. Compute the mean over the k^2 observations, say $\overline{f}(i, j)$ and the median using the same observations, say $\widetilde{f}(i, j)$, and return $g(i, j) = \alpha \overline{f}(i, j) + (1 - \alpha) \widetilde{f}(i, j)$ in every fit coordinate (i, j). If $\alpha = 1$ the filter reduces to the mean, and if $\alpha = 0$ it becomes the median. Intermediate values will retain part of the good properties of both filters. An excellent reference for this particular subject is the work by Arias-Castro and Donoho (2009)

Rather than using the median, the minimum and maximum values observed in the mask can also be employed. The former tends to leave the image darker, while the latter usually leaves the image lighter.

Notice in Fig. 5.10c that the result of these filters provides a kind of nonlinear envelope to the original data, and that small details have been completely removed.

(a) **(b)**

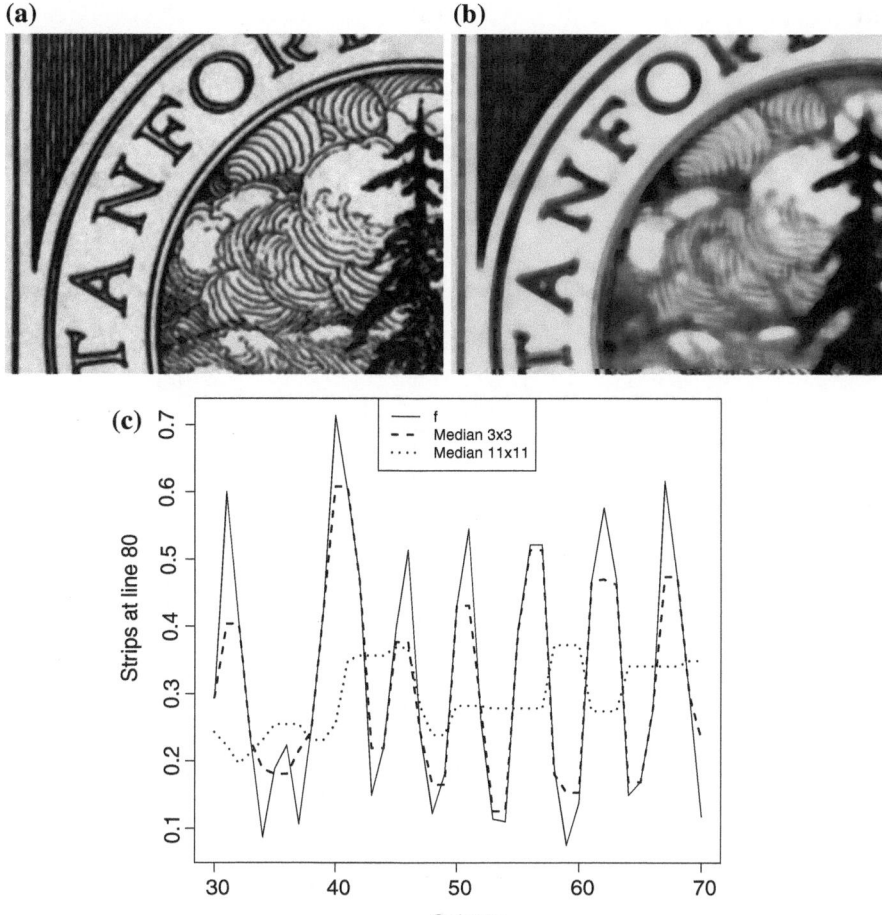

Fig. 5.9 Filtering with the median. **a** Mask of side 3. **b** Median of side 11. **c** Profiles at line 80

These operations form the basis of one of the most general nonlinear frameworks for signal and image processing: Mathematical Morphology (Shih 2009).

Order statistics can also be used in adaptive procedures, as the ones discussed by Lopes et al. (1990). Consider, for instance, the σ filter. It consists of estimating the mean $\bar{x}$ and standard deviation s on each window, and the computing the filtered value as the mean of only those observations which belong to the $[\bar{x} \pm ks]$ interval, with $k > 0$.

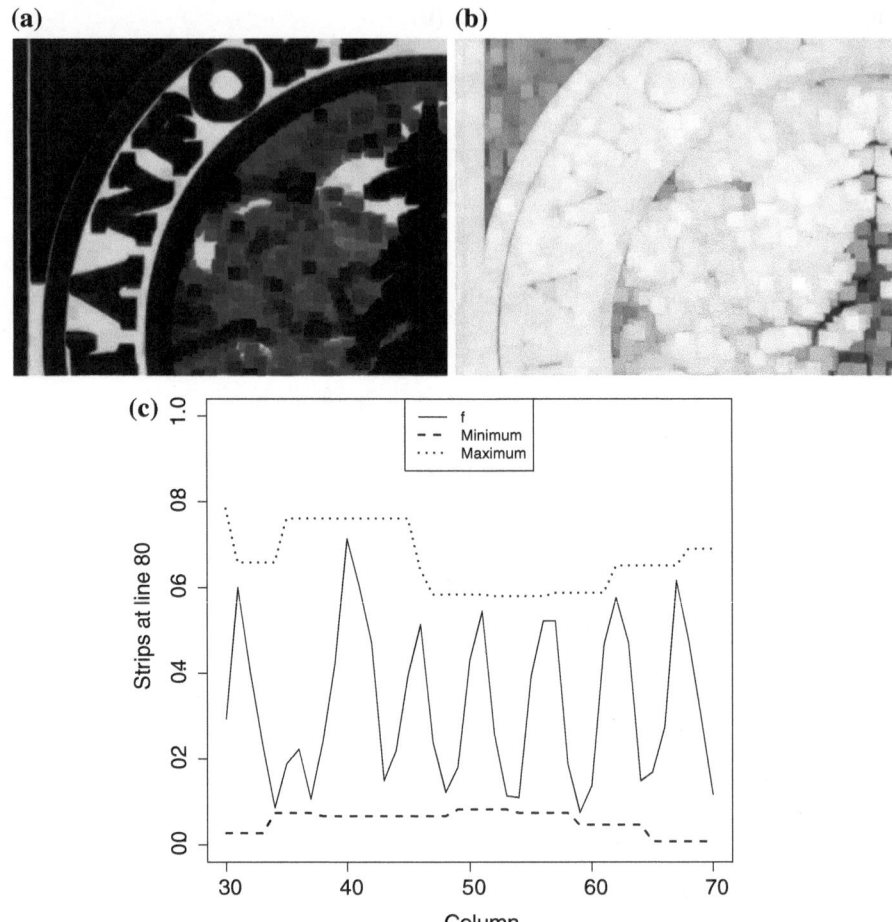

Fig. 5.10 Filtering with the minimum and the maximum on masks of side 11. **a** Minimum. **b** Maximum. **c** Profiles at line 80

References

Arias-Castro, E., & Donoho, D. L. (2009). Does median filtering truly preserve edges better than linear filtering? *Annals of Statistics*, *37*(3), 1172–1206.

Barrett, H. H., & Myers, K. J. (2004). *Foundations of image science*. Wiley-Interscience, NJ: Pure and Applied Optics.

Gonzalez, R. C., & Woods, R. E. (1992). *Digital image processing*. MA: Addison-Wesley.

Goudail, F., & Réfrégier, P. (2003). *Statistical image processing techiques for noisy images: an application-oriented approach*. Kluwer: New York.

Huber, P. J. (1981). *Robust statistics*. New York: Wiley.

Jain, A. K. (1989). *Fundamentals of digital image processing*. Englewood Cliffs, NJ: Prentice-Hall International Editions.

Lim, J. S. (1989). *Two-dimensional signal and image processing: prentice hall signal processing series*. Prentice Hall: Englewood Cliffs.

Lira Chávez, J. (2010). *Tratamiento digital de imágenes multiespectrales* (2nd ed.). Universidad Nacional Autónoma de México. URL http://www.lulu.com..

Lopes, A., Touzi, R., & Nezry, E. (1990). Adaptive speckle filters and scene heterogeneity. *IEEE Transactions on Geoscience and Remote Sensing, 28*(6), 992–1000.

Maronna, R. A., Martin, R. D., & Yohai, V. J. (2006). *Robust statistics: theory and methods*. Wiley, England: Wiley series in Probability and Statistics.

Medeiros, M. D., Gonçalves, L. M. G. & Frery, A. C. (2010). Using fuzzy logic to enhance stereo matching in multiresolution images. *Sensors, 10*(2), 1093–1118. URL http://www.mdpi.com/1424-8220/10/2/1093, (Special issue: Instrumentation, Signal Treatment and Uncertainty Estimation in Sensors).

Myler, H. R., & Weeks, A. R. (1993). *The pocket handbook of image processing algorithms in C*. Prentice Hall: Englewood Cliffs NJ.

Russ, J. C. (1998). *The image processing handbook* (3rd ed.). CRC Press: USA.

Shih, F. Y. (2009). *Image processing and mathematical morphology: fundamentals and applications*. CRC Press: USA.

Velho, L., Frery, A. C., & Miranda, J. (2008). *Image processing for computer graphics and vision* (2nd ed.). London: Springer.

Chapter 6
Contrast Enhancement and Dimensionality Reduction by Principal Components

There is no quality in this world that is not what it is merely by contrast. Nothing exists in itself.

Herman Melville

Figures 5.2 and 5.3 illustrate a characteristic common to almost every image: the data in different bands are correlated, i.e., there is redundant information. Strong positive correlation is translated into unsaturated colors, since points in the color space will not fill its volume; they will rather lie close to the diagonal which goes from black to white, yielding dull or pastel tones. Attempts to alleviate this issue by scale transformations in each band are quite limited.

In this chapter, we will see one of the most powerful transformations which enable reducing the correlation of data, leading to techniques which both allow performing contrast enhancement and data compression. The reader is referred to the book by Jackson (2003) and the references therein for more information about Principal Component Analysis.

The idea behind Principal Components consists in identifying the directions which best describe the data variation in the data space. For instance, in Fig. 5.2 none of the "natural" axes, i.e., the original bands, is a good descriptor. The best descriptors are straight lines (linear combinations) at about $\pi/4$ radians, notably in the "green-blue" projection. Once the good descriptors have been found, the data are projected onto them; these are the principal components. By construction, the data in the new space are uncorrelated. This operation is commonly referred to as PCA—Principal Component Analysis, and relies on the decomposition of the covariance matrix of the data.

Consider the multiband image $f : S \to \mathbb{R}^p$, with $p \geq 2$ and S a $m \times n$ Cartesian grid. It will be convenient to write explicitly each band, i.e., $f = (f_1, \ldots, f_p)$ with $f_i : S \to \mathbb{R}$ for every $1 \leq i \leq p$. The data in each band will be considered as a sample of size mn from a real random variable, and the observations in each pixel will be therefore described as a sample from a p-variate random variable $F : \Omega \to \mathbb{R}^p$.

A. C. Frery and T. Perciano, *Introduction to Image Processing Using R*, SpringerBriefs in Computer Science, DOI: 10.1007/978-1-4471-4950-7_6, © Alejandro C. Frery 2013

We will derive a linear transformation $\Psi : \mathbb{R}^p \to \mathbb{R}^p$ with good properties, i.e, we will find $G = \Psi(F)$. The resulting object $g : S \to \mathbb{R}^p$ will be an image.

Each element of each band in $g = (g_1, \ldots, g_p)$ will be of the form

$$g_i(s) = \alpha_i^1 f_1(s) + \cdots + \alpha_p^i f_p(s) \text{ for every } s \in S, \text{ so} \tag{6.1}$$

$$\boldsymbol{\alpha}^i = (\alpha_i^1, \ldots, \alpha_p^i), \tag{6.2}$$

where $\boldsymbol{\alpha}^i = (\alpha_i^1, \ldots, \alpha_p^i)$ are fixed real coefficients. Such transformation can be conveniently expressed in matrix form, i.e., $g = fA$, where f is the image data arranged as a $mn \times p$ matrix; any order can be used, a lexicographic one would be a good choice. The matrix A is formed by p vectors $\left(\boldsymbol{\alpha}^{1^\top} \ldots \boldsymbol{\alpha}^{p^\top} \right)$.

We are interested in finding a matrix A leading to a transformed image g with interesting properties; in particular, we would like the bands of g to be uncorrelated.

Assume the underlying distribution which characterizes F has the $p \times p$ covariance matrix Σ. Also assume this matrix is positive definite, so it can be decomposed into a matrix of eigenvectors A and a vector of eigenvalues Ξ. This means that $A\Sigma A^\top = \text{diag}(\Xi)$, where $\text{diag}(\Xi)$ denotes the operation that transforms a vector of dimension p into a matrix of dimension $p \times p$ with the values of Ξ in the diagonal and zero elsewhere. Now we will use the result presented in the Claim presented in page xx.

Provided we have the knowledge of Σ and, therefore, we know A and Ξ, if we make the linear transformation $G = FA$ the covariance matrix of G is, (page xx) $\text{Cov}(G) = \text{Cov}(FA) = A^\top\text{Cov}(F)A = A^\top \Sigma A = \text{diag}(\Xi)$ which, by construction, is a diagonal matrix. All the elements outside the diagonal of $\text{diag}(\Xi)$ are zero, so all pairs of bands of G are uncorrelated. Notice that one of the few cases for which "uncorrelated" also means "independent" is the multivariate Gaussian distribution, but in most situations lack of correlation does not lead to independence.

Back to Eqs. (6.1) and (6.2), the columns of the rotation matrix A are the eigenvalues of the spectral decomposition of the covariance matrix Σ, and they are the vectors $\boldsymbol{\alpha}^{i^\top}$, $1 \leq i \leq p$.

The elements of the diagonal matrix are $\Xi = (\xi_1, \ldots, \xi_p)$. They are the variances of each projection, i.e., of each band in G, and they are called the eigenvalues of the spectral decomposition of the covariance matrix Σ.

If we use the variance of each band as a measure of the information it conveys, the random variable F_i which describes the original band i provides a fraction equal to $\text{Var}(F_i)/\sum_{j=1}^p \text{Var}(F_j)$ of the total information. Should one be forced to choose a single band with the most information with this criterion, one should opt for the one with highest variance.

In practice, one does not know the true, underlying covariance matrix Σ, so it has to be estimated from the data.

Listing 6.1 shows the basic steps for reading and preparing the data for the PCA. Line 1 loads the `rgl` library which provides high-level interfaces to OpenGL routines; it is quite convenient for the interactive visualization of, for instance, points in a three-dimensional space. Line 2 reads the image, which is stored in a `imagematrix` matrix structure; the image is shown with the command issued in line 3, and the result is presented in Fig. 6.1a. Although the picture has a nice color balance, it is a good candidate for contrast enhancement by decorrelation due to the predominance of pastel tones. Figure 6.2a shows the original red, green, and blue bands. The matrix-like format, the data are stored, prevents the direct use of PCA routines, so lines 4 to 6 build a data frame with named variables, and line 7 makes them available outside the data frame. The boxplots labeled "red", "green", and "blue" in Fig. 6.3 present the boxplots of these three original bands; notice that they are quite "well-behaved", with no surprising values and similar distributions. Line 18 opens an interactive plot showing the image data in 3D, each point being a pixel painted with the color it appears in the image. The user can freely choose the viewpoint and angle, and when he finds an interesting perspective, line 19 freezes the output in a PNG file, shown in Fig. 6.4a.

Listing 6.1 Reading and preparing the data

```
1  > library(rgl)
2  > image <- read.jpeg("../Images/RussianFamilyOriginal.jpg")
3  > plot(image)
4  > bands <- data.frame(red = as.vector(image[,,1]),
5                        green = as.vector(image[,,2]),
6                        blue = as.vector(image[,,3]))
7  > attach(bands)
8  > var(bands)
9               red        green         blue
10 red     0.05892465  0.06113676  0.05634141
11 green   0.06113676  0.06736232  0.06395945
12 blue    0.05634141  0.06395945  0.06451329
13 > cor(bands)
14              red        green         blue
15 red     1.0000000  0.9703880  0.9138073
16 green   0.9703880  1.0000000  0.9702231
17 blue    0.9138073  0.9702231  1.0000000
18 > plot3d(bands, col=rgb(red,green,blue), pch=20)
19 > snapshot3d("../Images/Original3D.png")
```

Line 8 of Listing 6.1 computes and displays the covariance matrix of the original data. The reader is invited to verify that the formation content in each band, as measured by the variance, would lead us to choose the green band. It explains approximately 35 % of the total variance, while the blue and red bands carry 34 and 31 %, respectively. Line 13 calculates and exhibits the correlation matrix. It is noticeable how strong it is among all bands; it ranges between 0.91 (red and blue bands) and 0.97 (the other two pairs of bands). This linear correlation will be reduced to zero by the principal component transformation.

Line 1 of Listing 6.2 performs the Principal Components transformation. The scale and center options are the default, but in the code we stress that the data has to be centered and scaled prior to the transformation. It produces a structure, stored in pca_image, with a number of results whose summary is displayed with the command shown in line 2.

(a)   **(b)**

Fig. 6.1 Image before and after contrast improvement by decorrelation. **a** Original image.
b Enhanced image

Listing 6.2 Applying PCA

```
1   > pca_image <- prcomp(bands, scale = TRUE, center = TRUE)
2   > summary(pca_image)
3   Importance of components:
4                              PC1      PC2      PC3
5   Standard deviation      1.7039  0.29359  0.10304
6   Proportion of Variance  0.9677  0.02873  0.00354
7   Cumulative Proportion   0.9677  0.99646  1.00000
8   > (rotMatrix <- pca_image$rotation)
9                  PC1           PC2           PC3
10  red     -0.5735838  -0.706574658   0.4144320
11  green   -0.5848440  -0.001001234  -0.8111451
12  blue    -0.5735495   0.707637796   0.4126617
13  > (rotMatrix %*% t(rotMatrix))
14                    red         green         blue
15  red     1.000000e+00  -2.220446e-16   0.000000e+00
16  green  -2.220446e-16   1.000000e+00  -3.330669e-16
17  blue    0.000000e+00  -3.330669e-16   1.000000e+00
18  > bands_pc = data.frame(PC1 = pca_image$x[,1],
19                          PC2 = pca_image$x[,2],
20                          PC3 = pca_image$x[,3])
21  > boxplot(c(bands, bands_pc), horizontal=TRUE, notch=TRUE)
```

Line 8 of Listing 6.2 assigns and displays the rotation matrix, i.e., the eigenvectors
which perform the transformation. Line 13 shows that this is an orthonormal matrix:
the product with its transpose is the identity matrix (with negligible errors due to the
numerical representation of the data with finite precision).

Line 21 of Listing 6.2 produces Fig. 6.3. The boxplots labeled "PC1", "PC2",
and "PC3" describe the principal component data; technically, they are not bands
since there are values outside the [0, 1] interval. Notice that the second and third
principal components data are much more concentrated than the first one; c.f. line 5

(a)

(b)

(c)

Fig. 6.2 Original and transformed bands. **a** Original bands. **b** PCA bands. **c** Rotated bands

of Listing 6.2 for the standard deviation of each component. Once these data have been scaled, they are shown in the form of image bands in Fig. 6.2b.

The first principal component band (Fig. 6.2b, left) looks like the negative of any of the original bands. This can be explained by the fact that the first eigenvector of the transformation (first column of lines 10, 11 and 12 of Listing 6.2) are approximately equal, and all negative. Since the PCA matrix decomposition is invariant to changes of sign applied to all the components of each eigenvector, this means that most of the information is stored in the mean of the three original bands; in fact, as presented in line 7, the first principal component explains approximately 96.77 % of the total variance conveyed in the data. The amount of information contained in the other two principal components is drastically reduced: 2.87 and 0.35 %, respectively. The original bands, ordered by the variance, explained 35, 34, and 31 %, so discarding the two least informative would have led to loosing approximately 65 % of the

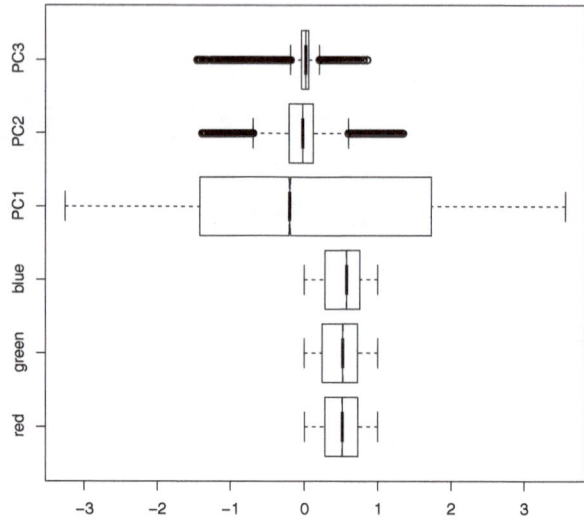

Fig. 6.3 Boxplots of the original (three from *bottom* to *top*) and transformed bands

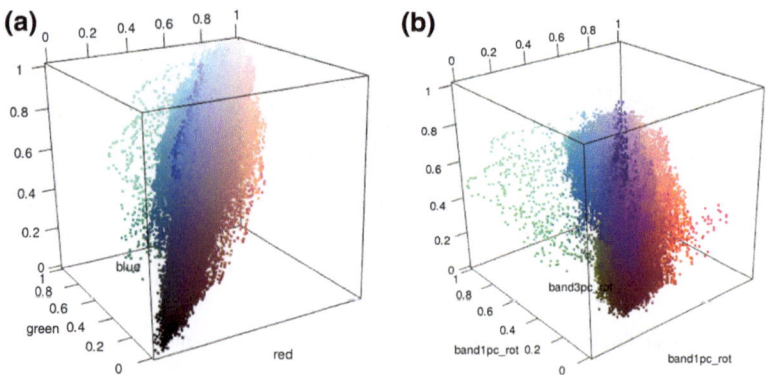

Fig. 6.4 3D visualization of pixels before and after contrast enhancement by decorrelation **a** Original bands. **b** Transformed bands

information, while doing the same with the transformed data would have discarded only about 3 %.

The results presented in line 6 of Listing 6.2 suggest one of the most important applications of the Principal Components transformation, namely, dimensionality reduction. When faced with the problem of choosing the linear transformation which conveys most of the variance (which can be understood as a measure of information content in some applications), the best choice is the first principal component. This procedure is of particular interest when dealing with remote sensing imagery, where the number of bands range from 7 to 250, and reducing the data dimensionality may lead to faster classification algorithms with negligible loss of information.

Listing 6.3 proceeds with the principal component analysis. We will use a stretch function, as the one defined in Eq. (5.1) and implemented in lines 1–8 of Listing 5.5 (page xx). In all following cases, the minimum and the maximum output values will be 0 and 1, respectively, so, for the sake of brevity, we will refer to this function as map01.

Listing 6.3 Applying contrast enhancement by decorrelation

```
1   attach(bands_pc)
2   bands_pc01 = data.frame(pc01.1 = map01(PC1), pc01.2 = map01(PC2),
3                   pc01.3 = map01(PC3))
4   attach(bands_pc01)
5
6   bands_stretch = as.matrix(bands_pc01) %*% t(rotMatrix)
7
8   result = data.frame(band1pc_rot = map01(bands_stretch[,1]),
9                       band2pc_rot = map01(bands_stretch[,2]),
10                      band3pc_rot = map01(bands_stretch[,3]))
11  attach(result)
12
13  image_pc <- c(band1pc_rot, band2pc_rot, band2pc_rot)
14  dim(image_pc) <- dim(image)
15
16  plot(imagematrix(image_pc))
17  plot3d(result, pch=19,
18          col=rgb(band1pc_rot, band2pc_rot, band3pc_rot))
```

The principal component bands have already been rotated, i.e., the data have been projected onto the axes along which there is most variation. Lines 2 and 3 stretch these data, and they now tend to fill the new data space... but this is not the original color space, so the hues are not preserved. Since we want to preserve the colors to some extent, we have to subject the stretched data to the inverse rotation. We already know that the inverse rotation is the transpose of the forward rotation (recall the result of line 13 from Listing 6.2); this is performed in line 6 (notice the as.matrix cast to the data frame structure). Nothing grants that after the inverse rotation the data lie within the $[0, 1]^3$ color space, so a new stretch is applied to each band independently while forming a new data frame; cf. lines 8–10 of Listing 6.3. Lines 13 and 14 transform this data frame into an image, which are subsequently plotted (line 16) and seen as points in the color space (lines 17 and 18). The results are shown in Figs. 6.1b and 6.4b, respectively.

It is interesting to compare the original and final bands. Notice that the former (Fig. 6.2a) are alike; only a very careful inspection reveals differences among them. The latter (Fig. 6.2c) exhibits variations which reflect on the more saturated colors. This is also clear comparing the 3D representation of the data, namely, Fig. 6.4a and b. The points in the latter span a bigger volume within the available color space and, as they lie further from the main diagonal, they produce more saturated colors.

Further reading on this subject is the books by Johnson and Wichern (1992); Jolliffe (2004); Krzanowski (1988, 1995); Krzanowski and Marriott (1995) and

Mardia, Kent and Bibbi (1982). The work by Muirhead (1982) is an authoritative reference for the most theoretical aspects of multivariate statistical analysis.

References

Jackson, J. E. (2003). *A user's guide to principal components*. Hoboken: Wiley.

Johnson, R., & Wichern, D. (1992). *Applied multivariate statistical analysis*. Nueva Jersey: Prentice Hall.

Jolliffe, I. T. (2004). *Principal component analysis* (*2nd* ed.). New York: Springer.

Krzanowski, W. J. (1988). *Principles of multivariate analysys: A user's perspective*, Oxford Statistical Science Series. Oxford: Claredon Press.

Krzanowski, W. J. (1995). *Recent advances in descriptive multivariate analysis*: *Royal statistical society lecture note series* (Vol. 2). Oxford: Claredon Press.

Krzanowski, W. J., & Marriott, F. H. (1995). *multivariate analysis: Classification*. London: Arnold.

Mardia, K. V., Kent, J. T., & Bibbi, J. M. (1982). *Multivariate analysis*. Londres: Academic Press.

Muirhead, R. J. (1982). *Aspects of multivariate statistical theory*: *Wiley series in probability and mathematical statistics*. New York: Wiley.

Index

A. C. Frery and T. Perciano, *Introduction to Image Processing Using R*,
SpringerBriefs in Computer Science, DOI: 10.1007/978-1-4471-4950-7,
© Alejandro C. Frery 2013